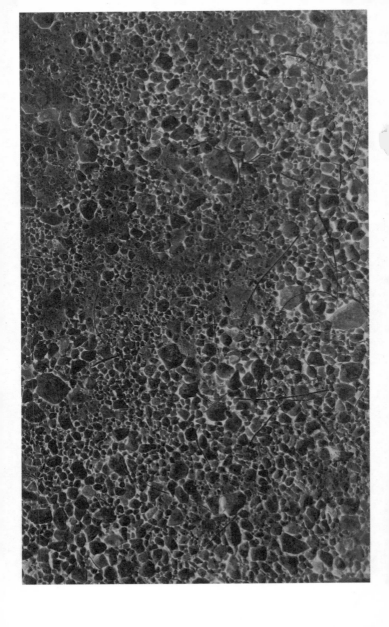

WITNESS B
DESMOND FAHY

Des Fahy

0358 Books

Published in 2015 by 0358 Books
32 Rosetta Avenue
Belfast
Email: 0358Books@gmail.com

A catalogue record for this book is available from the British Library.

ISBN: 978-0-9933379-0-1

Editing: Emma Warnock
Book design: Pony Ltd., London
Images: hoskingindustries.com.au
Printed in Ireland by Impress

To Paula, always

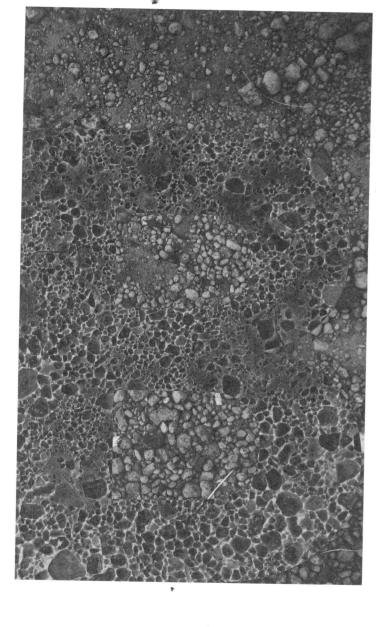

They called him Velcro Man. He hated that. Really fucking hated that. What sort of name was that to give anyone – Velcro Man? Not a lot of love there. Not much respect going on either. Still, what would you expect from that shower?

B struggled through the heavy double doors by forcing his mid-section – between the Racing Post under his arm and where his belt began – against one of the chrome, semi-circular handles. He could feel a sickly blast of hot air from above. Make the place seem warm and welcoming must have been the psychology once upon a time. What a waste of Barney's good money. None of the hopeless cases inside here needed that sort of encouragement. They would have preferred no heating at all, the more it seemed like hardship the better. Matched the general mood.

By now B had made it inside the betting shop. His perma-nervous eyes darted around the area between the door he had just come in, the bank of screens on his left, the newspapers displaying that day's form on the far wall and the first two betting windows along the right hand side. After that he couldn't really see. His glasses were old-fashioned, thick and Eric Morceambe-esque but could be doing with a bit of fine-tuning. Something else to do after he got Christmas out of the way.

Still, he could see enough to know that his entry hadn't raised a flicker of interest or a nod of recognition. How long had he been coming in here? He wasn't sure. But he knew that since he'd left work there had barely been a missed day or evening. This is what he did. Much more than where he lived, where he drank, where he got his Mass, this was now what defined him, who he was. And what did these bastards care? Velcro Man. Who's man enough to say it to my face? Who's man enough now?

He wasn't sure when it had started or who had first come up with Velcro Man, but that hardly mattered. If he was to drop dead right now or if there had been a bomb back in the bad old days, a handful would have been hard pushed to remember his name. Not able to place him they would have struggled until someone reminded them.

You'd know him if you saw him. Your man, Velcro Man. That's how it was. That's where he had finished up. They called him Velcro Man – what sort of fucking name was that?

It had been going on for years but he had never asked anyone what it was all about, this Velcro Man thing. Far, far too proud for that. Don't let yourself down in company, his mother had always told him. Don't be afraid of being different. It's good to be the odd one out. The odd one out, that just about summed it up. Take too much bad advice early on and this is how you can end up. What a warning.

B had never asked anyone, but he found out all the same. One June afternoon, in the days when it was the old shop, he was hiding down the back with all the other midsummer refuseniks studying Flat form for one of those posh English tracks. It was long enough ago for him not to have given into glasses and he was peering up at one of the pages from the Daily Mirror pinned up on the wall with those brass-coloured tacks you used to see in school. Now they're all sorts of fancy colours and shapes but back then a thumb tack was a thumb tack. He knew about these things, if anyone ever bothered to ask.

A five-furlong maiden was going to post, was it Bath or Windsor? What matter, it was somewhere posh and English anyway. He had nipped in between calls and was looking for a winner to tide him over until he got in later for a proper bet. The shop had kept its side of the deal with the four or five men scattered around keeping the amount of natural light and sunshine that escaped inside to a fitful minimum. They had come in to avoid the summer, not to bask in it. The only thing that defined the seasons in here was the presence or absence of fences – flat in summer, jumps in winter. Nothing else was needed.

Bits and pieces of a conversation from three pages down the line of the back wall floated towards him in the stale, hot air. There were two of them gathered around the inside page of the Irish News, half-gossiping and laughing and half-looking for a winner. One of them was a postman who did the round in the street next to his. A mouthy fella, he drank in the pub across the road and seemed to luxuriate in a job that finished at lunchtime and allowed him to flit back and forward from his half-and-half to his betting docket until it was time to go home for his tea. They didn't think he could hear them but he could. He didn't know the other man.

Do you see the cut of him? Look at the state of what he's wearing.

He could just make out a snorted reply, like someone swallowing a laugh and hoping that nobody else will notice. They were talking about him, the fuckers. There was nobody else around, it couldn't be anyone else. Pretending to study the newspaper page even more intently, he tried to remember what he had put on that morning without looking down in case they were watching him. Instinctively he wondered if there was a mirror or a glass door anywhere nearby that might help him out. No joy there, this was a bookies not a women's changing room in Robinson and Cleaver.

B steeled himself and threw his eyes downwards from the page and made a quick assessment starting with the shoes and moving up. The whole process took a second tops, two at the most. He wasn't about to give them the satisfaction of thinking he was worried about what they were saying. Brown canvas shoes. With black laces from his good pair in the cupboard under the stairs that only escaped for funerals and the Christmas mornings in Milltown. Light blue slacks with a black leather belt. Well, leather-effect anyway. A red tartan kind of plaid shirt. He didn't know all the fancy words and phrases. He'd seen a kilt like it once on some Scottish television programme. A yellow tie and a cream zip-up jacket, like you sometimes saw golfers wearing. Had he missed anything? No.

The bastarding postman was talking again in snorting, punctuated whispers. The bastard.

> The poor fucker....

The laughter was louder now, more obvious.

> Looks like he's covered himself in Velcro, closed his
> eyes and walked into his wardrobe. Whatever sticks to
> him that's what he wears for the day.

The two of them were now bent over, slapping each other on the back, and the man he didn't know was saying,

> Stop, he'll hear you, he'll fucking hear you.

He'd heard them alright.

> And then he gets up the next morning and starts the
> whole thing all over again.

They stumbled away, almost embracing now and delighted with their self-satisfying, impromptu routine.

They called him Velcro Man. That's why they called him Velcro Man.

What time is it? He'd come in to have two bets – the two o'clock and the 2.35 at Cheltenham. And the second one was the big one – the Paddy Power Chase. Some of the best jumpers in the country going at it, top-class racing, not like the Flat stuff, five furlongs, blink and you'll miss the charge. He had no problem with it, more than that, he was glad of it, during the summer when it filled in time. But it wasn't real racing, just not real enough for him. The Flat jockeys only had to get down to seven stone whatever and steer the horses round. To get round Cheltenham you had to be able to ride, to think your way round.

Look at McCoy. AP McCoy. The man's a genius, an awkward bastard they seemed to say in the papers, but a genius all the same. He could get horses home who didn't even know that they wanted to do it. That took balls. Balls and determination. And look at the size of him, almost six feet and still making those crazy weights. Leaning on the rail one day up near the front of the shop he'd heard two well-dressed boys, suits and fancy coats, talking about how he had to slim down to get on the best horses.

> He was in the back of a car once and the fella in the front was eating a packet of crisps. McCoy says, Give us one of those. Nobody could believe it, the champion jockey and all that, but they passed the bag back. Well you would, wouldn't you? And your man rummaged around in the bag until he could find the biggest crisp that was left. He took a good look at it, licked all the flavouring off, back and front, then wound down the window and threw it out. Would you credit that?

Even if it wasn't true, it was a good story. What he liked more than anything about McCoy was that he looked like he wanted to win even more than the boys who were ranting and roaring in the shop with their blue dockets in their hands. He never looked truly happy, like there was always something else to do, somewhere else to go and win. They liked that, appreciated him for that.

Anyway, what time is it? He pulled up his left jacket sleeve and pushed up the tartan shirt to where the watch should be. Nothing there. What time is it? Two hairs past a freckle. Where had that come from? School? Yeah, school. Somebody's smart answer. Wasn't there another one from then? What was it? What time is it? Time you got a watch. The old ones were the best.

What time is it? Where was his watch? He motioned as if he was frisking himself, padding first his trousers and then the pockets of his jacket in that semi-theatrical way middle-aged men do when they've lost something but are too vain and stupid to let anyone else know that they're actually looking for it.

Nothing doing. Must be beside the bed back at home. Or maybe on the shelf or the window sill in the bathroom. Or somewhere. He turned around to face down the shop and peered through his thick lenses at the screens to the right of the back wall's form pages. How many were there? 12, 14, 16? Fuck knows. A lot anyway. Far too many for sure. The digital clock in the corner of one of them read 1.46pm. Not too bad, plenty of time yet to get organised for the Juvenile Novices' Hurdle at 2. It was a real bookies benefit, take a chance and hope for the best with those youngsters, but there you go.

One of the bank of screens was showing pictures of the horses going down to the starting line at Cheltenham. It looked freezing there. Another was showing golf. Golf? What was the point of that? Posh bastards with more money than sense. There wasn't much golf in shops like this back in the day and better places they were too. A third, further down the row, was showing the end of a six-furlong handicap from Uttoxeter. A collection of nags if he ever saw one. They shouldn't allow that sort of rubbish on a day like today when the best of the chasers were out and about at Cheltenham. There was real business to be done and that was only getting in the way. Lining the pockets of those boys behind the counter, that's all that type of racing was for.

The rest of the screens were showing race odds and then results in various states of readiness, like so many plays running from the opening scene to their ends all at the same time.

TWO

This single drop of rain had been balanced on the edge of his nose for seven seconds. He knew that because he had counted into himself – one, two, three, four, five, six, seven. It was the only way he could keep his mind distracted from the sound of his breathing, the only way not to draw disastrous attention to himself. But now the water was starting to move, not much but enough for him to notice. The pull of gravity was moving it down his nostril, little by little. How long was it going to be before it fell from his nose on to his top lip? Five seconds? Ten? And what was he going to do then?

B thought about how stupid and ridiculous this must look but quickly bit on the smile in case that merest facial expression could be heard. Nobody must know he was here. Nobody. But it must look totally mad all the same. Like that thing that would happen to you on a cold morning on the way to work. You'd have your duffle coat, your bobble hat and your gloves all on to keep most of you warm but the exposed parts of your face couldn't escape and the invasive cold made little droplets on the edge of your nose. All you had to do then was wipe a gloved hand across and that was that, job done.

Here it was different. His arms were in the same position as when he'd jumped over the fence and laid himself out as close to the wooden slats and posts as he could manage. At one side of his body his left arm and hand were straight and rigid as if he were on some sort of impromptu parade and standing to obedient attention. And his right hand had somehow found itself knuckles down and palm up under his right thigh. While the left hand was now damp and cold, his right was being warmed by the heat of his body above it. As far as it went on this cold, cloudless night this self-generated heat was a good thing but the downward pressure of his body weight was now affecting the blood flow. The pins and needles had started off as a dull, barely-felt sensation, almost pleasurable in the way they had put him in touch with the internal workings of his own body. But now the curiosity was wearing off and the discomfort was becoming increasingly unbearable. If this went on much longer he was going to have to move and that was it.

He knew it was just plain stupid but he was starting to become consumed by the idea that his arm was going to fall off, going to become disconnected from his body as he lay there, rigid with a combination of fear and cowardice on the wet north Belfast grass. That couldn't happen. Could it? He quarter-smiled again, afraid for his life but for maybe the first time gloriously in touch with his own body. You stupid bastard. Stupid bastard.

Closing his eyes he concentrated on that right arm and on the part where the wrist broadened up towards the elbow. That was where the obvious blockage was, where the blood had found that it could go no further. Where did it go then? Back up his arm? Or did it just well up there waiting for normal circulation service to be resumed? He knew that if he could only move his fingers, just for a second or two, the activity would be enough to encourage the idle, disengaged blood back in. Breathing imperceptibly through his nose, he tried to wriggle his little finger, starting first with the bit between his bottom knuckle and his finger nail. The relief was immediate and palpable. He closed his eyes and thought he could see, as well as feel, the blood rushing gratefully back in. Now he was moving all of his little finger and then, one by one, he slowly began moving the rest.

His hand was now making a mini-fist as he pushed it back into his thigh, in and out, in and out, in and out. The dull ache began to ease a little but he didn't dare do anything else or shift his body position in case the noise might give him away.

How long had he been here? How long had it been since he'd thrown himself over this bloody fence and laid himself out flat as flat could be? How long had it been since his only thought was how to make himself invisible and disappear into the grass and rubble beneath him? A minute, an hour, a week, a year? What did it matter? He was here and he was afraid, afraid of what he had seen, afraid of what else he might see and afraid of what they thought he had seen. He was here and he was afraid – that was all there was. Nothing else. For now that fear would keep him awake and that would be enough. Everything in his body and in his head was trying to shut him down, to send him into defensive mode. Like a hopeless lost arctic explorer who rests to conserve energy as he waits to be rescued. Stay in the tent, don't move and hope for the best. Lie here on the wet ground, don't make a sound and hope for the best.

But all he wanted to do now was sleep. Sleep was safety, sleep was security. Sleep was away from here. It was a way to disappear and be forgotten. His eyelids, first his right but followed pretty much instantaneously by the left, were collapsing in on themselves. He enjoyed and savoured the short sensation of darkness and the escape it represented but he then blinked hard to bring himself back. Had he made a noise? Of course not, but he had to be sure. To get through this he had to take himself somewhere, find and concentrate on a better time. Where and when were you last happy? – he'd read that somewhere, maybe one of his ma's magazines or in a religion book as school. He knew what answer the Brother would have expected. When I felt close to Jesus. But that wasn't going to do. Last happy? Come on. Come on.

He was 10, maybe 11. They'd got the afternoon off school for the match and had been bussed across the city to the pitches beside the new motorway. It had been wet, he remembered that.

>> We'll have to play on the gravel. The grass is soaking, the teacher had announced from the top of the bus.

A collective groaned greeted him, an anticipation of the scrapes and scabs to come after the inevitable falls on the hard stone chippings.

>> It'll tighten you. Besides, these country boys won't know what's hit them. All they have are bogs to play on down there. And hardly a decent football between them.

It was cold, really cold. They'd changed into their gear and most of the boys were sitting hunched forward with the sleeves of their freshly laundered school jerseys pulled over their hands, the bottom halves stretched over their knees.

>> Fuck sake, sir, get the heaters on.

>> They don't work. And mind your mouth, whoever that was. Next bit of language and whoever I catch at it doesn't play. Understood?

>> Tops. Then we can stay on the bus out of the fucking cold.

>> Enough, boys. That's enough.

They were early. And because of the cold nobody was much in the mood to get off the bus and start the disorganised kick about that would pass as their warm-up. This was a day for being outside as little as possible – the game would be long enough as it was.

>> That must be them.

They craned curiously out of the windows at the old-fashioned bus that pulled up alongside them. The country boys were doing the same from theirs and it looked like the animals of one zoo enclosure staring back at the occupants of another.

>> Look at the shape of their haircuts. Have they no fucking barbers down there?

Without even realising it, he ran his hand back and forward over his tight, city crewcut and behind and in front of him his team-mates were doing the same. Them and us. Them and us.

>> Right, boys, that's enough gawping. Let's go.

They filed reluctantly up the bus and out the front door, the metal studs of their boots clack-clacking as they trudged down the three steps.

And then the memory was gone. Was that it? Nothing more? He closed his eyes tight, not to sleep this time, but to remember. Wasn't it funny how close those two things were? Falling asleep and looking back, two journeys. But still nothing came. Not a single detail about the match, where he played, what he scored, if he scored. Who won even? He couldn't be sure. The pictures which fed into the memories were gone. He had reached the end of the reel. All he was left with were the sounds. Clack-clack. Clack-clack. Clack-clack. What was that? He thought he'd heard a footstep on the other side of fence. Had he? And if he could hear them then maybe they could hear him. He held his breath until he thought he was going to burst out, but even though he strained hard he could hear nothing more. He was safe for now.

Like a child being restrained in a dentist's chair, his head was fixed and looking upwards. With clamped-open eyes he searched the night sky. Every now and then a cloud, milky grey, hurried across, but all he could see now were stars. Lots of stars. That was useful because he could tell you next to nothing about the night sky. But he knew someone who did – Johnny, the funny guy from down the end of the street. Not funny ha-ha, but funny peculiar.

Johnny had been saving his Green Shield stamps for months. Everyone knew he was doing it because he would torture them for theirs. Before long everyone on their street and the two or three streets around knew about Johnny and his stamps. It had started off as a joke before mutating into an annoyance and Johnny continued to pester everyone he met.

> Don't forget, if you've any of those aul' stamps, missus, just send them my way. Johnny'll take them, don't you worry yourself about that.

People got curious and began to wonder what it was all about.

> What are you saving them for anyway, Johnny,

something big?

You'll see, you'll see.

He smiled as he answered, half-enigmatically, half-vacantly, as if something very important was — and was always going to be – missing. But then a strange thing happened. Almost without realising it, Johnny's neighbours stopped saving the stamps for themselves and began putting them to one side for Johnny. After the big weekly shop women would stuff the stamps into a side pocket of their purse with only Johnny in mind. At the filling station men who never bothered with them before found themselves asking for the stamps after they had paid for their petrol. What had started off as the street joke had now become a local obsession.

Come on, Johnny, here's some more of those stamps for you. What are they for anyway?

You'll see. You'll see.

After a while, it became the only thing anyone wanted to talk about.

Better than a soap opera, someone had said. He must have hundreds of them now.

And the rest. I hear he's putting his order in soon. What do you think he'll get? What in the name of God is he saving for? A Teasmade or one of those heated trolleys for his ma?

Or maybe something for himself. You'd never know with that boy. One of those Bullworkers to build himself up a bit. He's a puny wee runt at the same time, isn't he?

And so it went on and on. Eventually, just when everyone's curiosity was starting to get the better of them, a white van pulled up on the street. The driver and the delivery boy sitting in the front beside him were looking for number 17.

Who wants to know?

I've something for him from the airport.

Alright, just down there then.

Word spread quickly and a small cluster of people gathered on the other side of the street opposite Johnny's house. The delivery boy got out and knocked the front door twice. Johnny took an age to answer it and the watching crowd got impatient.

Come on. What's keeping him?

Slowly the door eventually opened. Johnny wasn't in any mood to rush his big moment. He scrawled his name on the clip-board which had been thrust in front of him. The delivery boy then disappeared behind the back double-doors of the van before re-emerging with a long tube-shaped cardboard box. Johnny took it from him, looked triumphantly first across the street and then back at the box before turning on his heels to go back inside.

What's in the box, Johnny? Come on, let the cat out of the bag.

Johnny stopped. This was his moment. His day in the local sun. He sucked some air into his cheeks, puffed himself out and cocked his head back over his right shoulder towards his expectant public.

It's a telescope. A telescope.

And then he was gone with a confident strut through the front door which clicked closed behind him.

A telescope. A telescope.

Some of the watching women rolled the word around in their mouths to get used to the wonder and strangeness of it all. A telescope.

A telescope. I told you he was wired up, a total one hundred per cent mad bastard. I always said he was a bit touched, him and the rest of his family.

What is there to look at around here anyway? We haven't got that much sky and what's there is full of helicopters.

Wired up, he is, you're right. Fucking wired up.

THREE

Everything changed in such a short space of time. Nothing stayed the same for very long. He liked that about this place, the transience, the sense that different times, maybe better times, were just around the corner. The idea that everything was possible, that you didn't just have to sit and take it. A few pen marks on a small, blue betting slip promised everything even if it delivered nothing in the end. Better to travel than to arrive, wasn't that what one of the teachers in school had said? He probably didn't have a place like this in mind, but there you go.

It was around the time when they opened the new shop. Steve Bruce, that football fella, had come to do the cutting of the ribbon. He remembered that. He'd been in that day, just to see what was going on, and wasn't there a photo somewhere on the wall near the front door? Steve Bruce and some of the boys from behind the counter. They all looked a bit older now. Did he? Never been a great man for photographs, didn't like getting his picture taken. Why was that? Too shy? Too awkward? There was a box somewhere in the house he'd taken from his mother's after she'd died with old pictures in it. They hadn't been looked at for an age. That would be something to do some day. Some day soon.

He'd loved those blackboards, still missed them if truth be told. The biggest one had stood in the middle of the shop facing the tills. Hanging from two chains like one of those big pictures in the old films they used to watch on Sunday afternoons. What did they have now? Plasma screens, was that what they were called?

There was a wee guy who stood there all day chalking up and rubbing out the different prices. In his short-sleeved shirt and his teacher's trousers, with tell-tale dust round the pockets. He had a wee ear-piece in his ear for the radio which kept him constantly up to date with the changing prices. With each new piece of information he'd move self-importantly back and forward making the necessary changes. Outside he was small and inconsequential, you'd walk past him in the street, barely nod to him at his pub table. But in here he was someone. When he chalked up people paid attention. You could tell he liked it, something in the way he subconsciously walked on his toes to make himself half an inch taller. What was his name? Sean? Jim? No matter, it'd come to him. Where had he finished up? You used to see him working the pay-out till but not so much these days. When they took away his blackboard, they took away a part of him. When it had gone he had to lose the half-inch and slink back down to where he'd come from.

But he could work the board, no doubt about that. It was like one of those acts you used to see at the circus, six plates spinning in the air at the same time, always on the brink of falling apart, always just managing to hold it all together. Success and failure running together.

The set-up was always the same. There would be small, A4 printed pages with the racecard for each track. Beverley. Musselburgh. Cartmel. Even the names were fantastic. He loved to roll them around in his mouth, places he had never been to and would probably never see. One hundred trips to make before you die! The wonders of the modern racing world! He had the same thing about the Destinations

15

board at airports – like a wish-list for the stay-at-home traveller, jet-setting for people with high hopes but less money. Let's look at what you could have won. Anyway. The white pages would be stuck to the top of the board. Like a reference point, a control tower for the activity that would unfold below them. Underneath, each race at each track would be chalked up in turn. Tiny, intricate writing, everything in its place and a place for everything. He used to think it impossibly beautiful, like some old book full of fancy flourishes and designs, almost within reach but always just too far away.

Using the A4 page, each race, when its time came, would be marked up in chalk until, just before the start of racing for the day, each opening race would occupy its own little space on the board. As the odds ebbed and flowed the necessary adjustment would be made with a swish of the wet cloth and a flurry of chalk marks. After the off of each race, the chalk-speckled rag moved swiftly across the board to confine that race to history and the calligraphic odyssey began all over again. There was a discernible, comforting rhythm to it all, like history being written, assimilated and then re-written every fifteen or twenty minutes. Life was mapped out in the time it took to get one race completed and the next one started. The cycle was pre-ordained and certain.

Once the race had been run and the list of runners and prices wiped away, it was like it had never existed. Not really. Like a distant memory you hold of your first day at school or the bike you got for Christmas, a small fragment was allowed to remain in the Results Section in the bottom corner of the board. But even that seemed like an afterthought. The writing was smaller and only the names of the placed horses, usually three and sometimes four, were preserved. For the rest, the race had been run and they were gone.

So the ritual continued through the afternoon and into the early evening, from lunchtime to going-home time with hardly a break in between. If the board man was lucky the gap between two races might allow a snatched half cup of tea or a quick run to the toilet but beyond that there was no discernible break.

There were times when it looked like it might become too much for him, as if the constant flurry of information was going to overwhelm the entire operation. But it all worked out in the end. On a busy Saturday afternoon, say round about half two, it was a wonder to behold. A constant turnover of names and prices being written and re-written, each one of them carrying maybe a day's, a week's or half-a-lifetime's cash-hard dreams.

And then they were gone. Like that children's story of the young girl out catching butterflies in reverse. Nothing could be kept for posterity. There was a terrible, in-built obsolescence to it all. Now you see it, now you don't. Hold on to what you can. Let's see what you could have won, let's see what you could have won.

> Alright?
>
> Not so bad. Yourself?
>
> Aye, alright.

This was as affectionate and warm as greetings got in the shop. And so it went on.

> Any luck?
>
> Just in. Thinking about doing one or two. Yourself?
>
> Some fucking chance. Backed one there at Lingfield. Four legs only made him dangerous. Bastard might still be running for all I know.

What was this guy's name? His name? It would come to him. It would come to him. Tom? Tommy? That was it. Tommy. They had been on nodding terms for years – acquaintances not friends as they'd put it one of those posh books – and had exchanged nothings of conversations like this one all that time without one ever finding out a single, significant thing about the other. The unspoken agreement and understanding was that they both preferred it this way. Keep yourself to yourself and nobody gets hurt. Never give too much away and there won't be too many problems.

What was that thing called on the radio in the mornings? With the priests and the ministers. Thought for the Day. He'd heard one a while back, some priest who'd rambled on for a bit and then got to the end. And doesn't that just go to show you that you can never have too many friends to call upon in your hour of need, with Jesus at the top of the list. What a load of balls, he remembered thinking. You've got a friend in Jesus and all that bollocks. Hadn't seen him about much recently. He'd enough friends, thank you very much, the fewer people knew about him the better for everyone. Interfering and nosy, most of them. Keep yourself to yourself and you can never go too far wrong. Secrets are for keeping.

In one of his blacker moods his father had told him once. If you have two good friends by the time you get to fifty you'll be doing well. Two? Chance'd be a fine thing. Still it was better than the opposite, the other side of the coin. Everybody knowing your business, your secrets and your past. Couldn't be doing with that. Danger there for sure. The past was where it belonged. Who'd want to go back there, back to all of that? He was happier where he was, thanks very much.

> Were you in yesterday?
>
> Aye.
>
> Didn't see you.
>
> Naw.
>
> What time were you in?

Jesus what was this, 20 Questions and a prize for the winner? Let's see what you could have won.

> Around lunchtime.
>
> Did you stay long?
>
> Naw. Just two bets and then on home.
>
> Any joy?
>
> Second and the other one was nowhere.
>
> I had bad luck now.

Here we go. Tell me something I don't want to know.

> Two up and waiting for a third in a treble for about 150 quid. Just touched off at the line by one of the Pipe's.
>
> Bastard.

The names of the horses, the jockeys and the trainers changed but the story stayed the same. Always one result away from a big win.

Always one number away from a fortune on the Lottery. Let down by the ground, the stupid fucking jockey, a fixed race or just plain honest to God bad luck. Roll up, roll up, take your pick, any excuse that takes your fancy. But as long as the prize was there, just out of reach, so close you could almost touch it, there was hope. The alternative was too awful to think about. A day, days, without hope, that didn't hold out a big 16/1 winner, a run of results that all went your way. It was why they bought into the illusion, why they played their roles dutifully in the communal charade and came back the next day with a cheap blue pen tucked behind one ear to do it all over again. The great big lie of success, of happy outcomes for everybody. They're all giving it a go. If you're not in you can't win. Why don't you give it a whirl? Let's see what you could have won.

By now the conversation had settled into the same rhythm and pattern as the countless other bland exchanges they had been part of over the years. One talking much more than the other – him not B – asking questions that were never properly answered but then never taking the obvious signals being sent out by the monosyllabic replies. Eye contact, as usual, was non-existent as both of them stared vacantly into space. It would have been a good test to ask one the colour of the other's hair and if he wore glasses or not. Both would have been hard pushed to answer, or at least would have needed time to think about it.

If he never saw Tommy again and never spoke to him again it would be too soon. But he played along with the social pretence because life was easier that way, less fuss and no hassle. Just how he liked it. And if life just now was about anything it was that – no hassle can only be a good thing.

But still it went on.

> Did you get your money stuff sorted out?
> What?
> You know, with the Social and your dole or whatever it was?

How did he know about that? What bastard had been talking

about him? Could you not keep anything private around here anymore? Was there no such thing as privacy?

Ah, that, aye. There's no problem. All sorted.

Glad to hear that. When those bastards get their claws into you it can be hard to get away. There's plenty in there in the Brew just dying to take it off you. You'd think it was their own fucking money, that it was them writing cheques out of their own accounts. There you are now, I'm glad to hear that, really glad, never like to hear about anybody in trouble like that. Because it can finish up in court, so it can. Good to hear some good news for a change. Not much of it around here these days.

Was he finished? Please God he was. Was that it? The two of them stood staring at the screen fixed to the wall in front of them for another while, like two pilgrims staring up at a statue and hoping for a sign, a blinding flash of light that would tell them everything was going to be alright. It didn't come. It never did in here. He moved across a couple of steps to his right and sat down in one of the red, bucket-shaped plastic seats at the end of the row right in front of the screen that was showing golf prices. He was close enough almost to touch it. Don't sit too close to the television, his mother had told him, it'll make your eyes go funny. Was that really right or just another lie to add to the rest?

There was no-one beside him and as far as he could tell no-one sitting behind him. Good. Anything to get away from the rubbish he'd had to put up with. He was still annoyed, really fucking cross, because he hated the idea of people talking about him, just hated it. Nothing better to do in their empty lives. It was a real struggle but what he had to do now was to pretend to be interested in the golf screen he was staring at. A man who looked like he was studying hard, not to be talked to. The funny thing was, he never touched the golf. For a start it took too long. Four days watching and waiting to see if you're were going to get any money back. Only the cricket took longer than that. What were the four days all about? The five minutes odd it took to finish a three-mile chase was just about his limit.

Even the Grand National went on too long for him, but then that wasn't a proper race anyway. Don't get him started about that. The shop was full all day with people he didn't know and who didn't know what they were doing. The queues were too long and worst of all the race was too unpredictable. No room for skill and knowledge there, stick in a pin and take your chance. Let's see what you could have won. Four miles plus around that track and those fences – how were you supposed to figure that one out?

> Three 50ps each way for the kids and 25p each way for granny. Where do I write it?

Jesus, give me strength. It just wasn't right that people would finish up where they didn't belong, were watching things that had nothing to do with them, were trying to understand something they should never have been exposed to. A place for everything and everything in its place, that's how it should have been. A place for everything? Was that how it went? Jesus, his head was full of some rubbish. Blame the parents, I blame the parents.

FOUR

His ma and da would be wondering where he was by now. Not just wondering, worrying as well. He'd already missed his tea and his ma would have been the first to notice that.

> Here he is, regular as clockwork. I should set my watch by you, you know, as she heard his key turning in the front door. No need for me to time the dinner when you're around. You'll always keep me right.
>
> Give over, ma. I'm a growing boy and need it all.

And then they would smile at the same time but without looking at each other, their two mutual loves colliding somewhere in the middle of the kitchen.

They'd be worrying now, alright.

> It's not like him at all. You know how fond he is of his food.
>
> I know, his da would reply from out in the hall trying not to sound concerned.

Because it would be his da, funny enough, who would be more uptight than his ma. He was sure of that. Only a while ago he'd warned him about looking after himself when he was out at night.

I know what's out there and I don't think your ma has much of a clue. Best to keep it that way, he'd said in the closest they had ever got to a conspiratorial father and son chat.

It's really not like him and if he doesn't get here soon it's going to be totally spoiled.

I know, I know. But talking about it's not going to make it happen. Best thing is not to fuss, we'd have heard if there was anything up.

He hoped he wasn't laying on the reassurance too thick.

Eat up your dinner. He'll be here in a minute.

If there was something wrong he'd have phoned, wouldn't he. Or at least somebody would have. But what if he couldn't get to a phone. What if somebody had got hold of him already.

For some reason, just after work, around tea-time, was their favourite time for trying to pick boys up off the street. Plenty of them about, was probably the thinking. Bound to get hold of one of them without anyone noticing. He'd always warned him, always tried to help him keep himself safe without scaring the wits out of him completely.

There's plenty of trouble about if you go looking for it. You know that and you don't need an old man like me to tell you. Keep your head down. Don't speak to anyone you don't know and don't make eye contact if you don't have to. It's all simple stuff, common sense and you must have picked up a wee bit of that from me, I hope.

Not from your side anyway.

Cheeky blurt.

His ma had given him the softer version of the same speech and he'd told her the same thing, don't worry, don't be getting yourself all worked up. Who would be interested in him anyway? Nobody. But that was the problem now. They had plenty of reason to be interested in him, especially if they knew what he had seen and where he was now hiding.

Ten seconds either way would have made a huge difference. Twenty at most. If only he'd crossed the street to get cigarettes or a paper when he'd thought about doing it and not decided to wait until he got up closer to the house. That would have killed enough time and kept him away from being where he was now at the wrong time.

> Just the paper, son?
>
> Aye and 10 Regal Red.
>
> Not a bad night.
>
> Naw.

An exchange of pleasantries and small talk wouldn't have cost him a second thought. A lifetime of listening to his ma had made him an expert, an A student. And it would have kept him back just long enough not to have arrived just when he did. Even if he'd got the bus. Or gone for a pint. Or stayed on to finish that wee bit of work. Or stopped to tie the laces on his boots. Anything, anything at all to cheat and steal another half minute out of the day. That was all he would have needed. How much was that to ask?

How often had he heard it on the news or read it in the paper. The dead man was simply in the wrong place at the wrong time. He'd never really thought about it before, this new vocabulary that everybody had learnt and was using. The innocent victim. Never a bad word to say about anyone. A devoted family man. With this new terror came a new language to describe it. Words whose meaning was just a little detached from reality but which washed over the people they were aimed towards like spring rain. He had never paid any attention to them because he had never had any need to. Nobody in his family had been shot or blown up; he hadn't yet been touched, even obliquely, by the evolving, enveloping tragedy. But now it had come looking for him and found him for fuck's sake. He was the man in the wrong place at the wrong time. They could put that in the paper about him. The living cliché. Or the dead one.

What if he had been a bit quicker out of work, had been past all of this before it had even happened? Then he could have attached himself to another part of this emerging language, the man with the lucky escape. He could have made the headlines if he was stupid enough to tell anyone all about it.

Isn't that on your way home? His da would have asked when it was all reported on the television news.

Aye, I suppose so.

You had a lucky escape there, so.

I didn't see any of it. He was looking at the policemen and the body bag and the ambulance. It must have been after I went past there.

The lucky escape. The lucky man. The jammy fella. He didn't much feel like that now, lying rigid still, his features stuck to the bones of this face and beginning to freeze where they had come to rest. Really fucking freezing cold. If this was lucky, his ma would never want him to walk her down to the bingo again.

And if he had been early, just a bit ahead of himself, would he have looked back to see what the noise, the shouting, then the shot and then more shouting was all about? What would he have done? In the toss-up between the good Samaritan and the coward safely on his way home for his tea, there was no contest, none at all. Not in these times and not on these streets. His da was right all along. Keep your head down. All the career advice a boy needs.

You're such a lucky bastard. That's three times in a row now.

That lunchtime, what was it, four or five hours ago now, they'd been playing pitch and toss with still-shiny, new halfpennies in the small yard at the back of the works. Surrounded on three sides by high, red brick walls it was the perfect arena, their own pitch and toss amphitheatre. Same as they did every lunch break, something to pass the time. Working men with very little gambling away what they had. And when the apprentices and new boys were a bit older they would leave such youthful foolishness behind and graduate to the betting shop with its own rituals of odds, pencils and dockets.

That's not luck, hey, skill that is, pure skill.

B smirked as he stooped down to collect first his coin, which was wedged tight against the wall, and his winnings, Brendan's effort, which had come to rest just a bit further back.

I'll wipe that smile off your face, you wee bollocks. Come on, let's go again.

The two men went to their mark, the imaginary line between the down-spouts which faced each other as they ran down from either side of the roof high above. B loved the sport of all of this, the fun of it, the messing. And he liked the uncertainty, that part of him that didn't know what was going to happen next. A game of chance, a game where anything could happen and there was very little you could do about it.

In a matter of seconds real life and the same old certainties would hurtle back towards him but for now he was somewhere else, somewhere a little further away. He revelled and immersed himself in the freedom and carefreeness of just not knowing what was going to happen next.

Have you enough left to play? I don't want you running back home to your missus this evening with your pockets empty and getting a row from her. She'll be looking for the housekeeping for the week.

Just play, you bollocks, just play.

He knew he'd got inside Brendan, same as he always could, and wasn't going to let the moment pass. Brendan looked sideways at him and just couldn't help himself.

Don't you worry about me, young fella, just play.

Brendan had been very good to him when he'd first arrived, straight out of school and knowing less than nothing. He'd looked after him and kept him right. He hadn't needed to but he had.

Don't forget, I know your da. There was a lot less lip out of him when he was here. If you're half the man he was you'll be doing alright.

Both men stood alongside each other turning their coins over in their fingers, like poker players about to place their bets.

You're up, big man. I won the last.

Think I don't know that, you sarky wee bastard. Watch and learn.

Brendan was crouched over now, a swimmer on his blocks about to launch himself. The coin rested on the nail of his dessert-spoon thumb and after one last glance towards the wall about twelve feet away he flicked it against his index finger. There was the faintest of noises, a gentle swish like a boy trying and failing to click his fingers in imitation of something he'd seen his father doing.

The halfpenny turned over on itself repeatedly so that you couldn't see which side was up as it moved noiselessly through the air. Both men watched.

Go on. Go... Brendan spoke but he hadn't meant to and he stopped himself.

It was only a wee game of pitch against the young lad for God's sake. The copper coloured circle struck the wall about eight inches from the wall, just as he'd intended, rebounded back and shimmered on the gravelly ground before coming to rest about three inches away.

You wee dancer. That's how it's done, young fella.

He wasn't even trying to hide his triumphalism.

Not bad.

Come on then, what have you got?

Leave me be. You can't hurry a pro, you know.

By now a few of the other lunchtime refuseniks had gathered around to watch. They smiled at the young man's impudence and cheek.

B had a plan, not much of a plan but a plan all the same. It was something that would really get Brendan going.

Watch now how it should be done.

Eyeing up the wall and the coin nestling not very far away from it, B flicked his high into the air, high, high, higher than normal. Just as he wanted.

Jesus that'll have snow on it when it comes down.

27

The coin seemed to hang forever in the air. B rocked involuntarily forward, willing it on. This time it didn't hit the wall at all. Instead it flopped straight down and landed with a clink on top of Brendan's, knocking his to the side before spinning once and settling in the very spot where the wall met the ground.

Perfect, B muttered under his breath. Just perfect.

Like a singer milking the audience for all they were worth at the end of a concert, B stood where he was. For a few seconds he was somewhere else, somewhere better, somewhere things worked out just like you wanted. Always. He had closed his eyes and when he opened them Brendan was standing in front of with his arm outstretched and both coins resting in his big, gnarled open hand.

Not much I can do about that. You're some wee bollocks, alright. Time to go back inside.

It's all in the flick, Brendy, it's all in the flick.

It's all in the flick. Pushing his thumb gently into the back of the knuckle of the finger squashed beside it, B made the same action over and over again. Back and forward. Back and forward. Practice makes perfect. What was that bit of his finger called? The knuckle? Aye it was the knuckle, but the back of the knuckle? In behind the knuckle, but further up too. Close to the joint. Maybe that was it. The joint?

He thought he could feel sand in between his fingers. Was it sand or gravel? Too small for gravel he decided, must be sand. Definitely sand, too smooth for gravel as well. There wasn't a lot of it, not like on a beach or something like that, but there was enough for him to know what it was. They must have been using it to lay a pavement or fix the road on the other side of the fence and some of it had blown over.

Who was it that didn't like sand? Not on his fingers or his hands, but in between his feet. Who was that? His wee brother, the wee man. Without fail he would complain about it, as a baby, when they went on their holidays down at the sea. And then one day it all came together. He just didn't care anymore and after a while he couldn't get enough of it, you couldn't get him away from it. A bucket and spade and he was ready to go.

Those holidays had been brilliant. Some posh relations of his ma's rented a house down there for the summer and they let them have two weeks, just after the July fortnight, for free.

> Couldn't beat that, his da said. You know me, I love a bargain.

> That's enough, tutted his ma back. Just be grateful and don't be making a show of me in front of them.

His ma took them up for the first week and his da followed at the weekend and then stayed for the second. They'd get the bus – what a carry-on – and his da would follow down on the Friday evening bus after work. They did that any time they got the chance. It became an old routine but treasured all the same. The shared memories of those holidays lit up their family memories like street lights.

Rituals had developed over time. Who got their bath first. Whose turn it was for a story. Who got first go at the towel after they'd scurried out of the freezing sea as if running towards just-burning toast. And then there were the breakfasts. When they got up to maybe nine or ten they'd be allowed to take a turn at cooking while the rest of them were away at eight o'clock Mass. It was her little way of getting them ready, preparing them for the life rolling out in front of them.

In time, B's day duly arrived. His big breakfast. The bonus of missing Mass was tremendous but the pay-off – breakfast for everyone – was plain terrifying.

> Make sure it's nice now, giggled one of his sisters as she took her place in the familial duck procession, with its nudging, pushing and jostling as they made their way towards the chapel.

What age was he then? Eleven, maybe twelve at most. That explained a lot. The forty-five minutes or so that they were away were filled mostly with inert fear and apprehension as he struggled to get to grips with what had to be done. And then it was only five minutes before they were due back. The squeaking open of the front door, followed a few seconds later by the gaggle of children talking all at once and over each other, sent his heart through the floor.

Let's see what he's got. I'm starving.

Boys, leave your brother alone, give him some room to think.

He remembered every detail. The children ate off garish blue and red plastic plates, bought by his ma in some special offer for a never-realised camping expedition. And she had a white plate with some kind of Chinese pictures along the outside and in the middle. They were blue as well, but a different kind of blue. Prettier. He now knew it was called china blue.

As he passed the plates in from the kitchen through the serving hatch to the big dining-room table with as much sense of ceremony as he could muster, there were immediate catcalls of derision followed by squeals of mock indignation.

I'm not eating that.

I thought this was supposed to be breakfast.

Piled up on each plate were as many baked beans as he could crowd on. They were lukewarm, too, because he hadn't left himself enough time to heat them up. And circled artlessly around the outside of the plates and surrounding the beans like cowboy wagons were quartered cold tomatoes.

The toast is coming.

Aye, so's Christmas.

Too scared to grill or fry anything, he'd remembered seeing beans served up for breakfast on the American Saturday morning programmes he watched on TV. The problem was that they'd never appeared on their family breakfast menu before.

Beans, ma, come on. What's this all about?

Leave him be, he's done his best.

The final indignity didn't come until years later. Around the table at Christmas dinner the famous seaside baked beans breakfast came up in conversation, too much communal grumbling and laughter.

You were lucky, his ma said, smiling at everyone but at

the same time making conciliatory eye contact with him. You didn't have to drink the tea. Everything looked alright but when I put the milk in and took a drink, well, he'd forgotten to boil the kettle, hadn't he? And I couldn't not drink it or push it away. Especially after you lot had done your best to finish him off as a chef forever.

And look how well that worked. He doesn't have to lift his hand.

Leave him be, leave him be.

FIVE

Tiger Woods was 20/1 to win all four Majors. Was that good value, a good bet? Who knows? He'd never got golf, but then again he was probably not the sort of person who was ever supposed to get golf. A game for stuck-up posh boys, he heard his father say one night from behind his paper. One of the few things he ever got right, God help him.

Somebody had said in the shop the other day that there were far more ordinary people taking it up these days. More of the other side too.

> The clubs needed the money, you see, with all the posh old boys dying off and nobody stepping into their empty plus fours, or whatever you called those stupid fucking Rupert the Bear trousers.

Not a game for him though, not at his time of life anyway. Maybe that was his biggest problem with the game, the stupid trousers they all seemed to wear. Had they no shame, those boys? More money than sense, anyway.

Test yourself. Name three famous golfers. Nicklaus, Palmer, Trevino.

Easy peasy. But they were old guys and it was never off the TV back then. You had to have cable now, or Sky. Name three modern players, if you're such a smart fella. Alright. Woods. Simple. Come on, another one? He was stuck. Who was the Irish fella whose wife died? I'm fucked if I can remember his name but. Come on, keep going, keep going. Shit. I'll get it, I'll get it. Ok, Give up. Give fucking up.

This was happening more and more, he was starting to realise. These voices, always with teasers, questions he'd heard before but just couldn't answer. And couldn't ignore either. The questions wouldn't go away until you came up with some way of answering them. Sometimes he'd say anything, just the first thing that came into his head and even if it wasn't right, just to bat the ball back to them, to the voices. Everything was starting to get mixed up as well, tied up with old memories, stuff he thought he'd forgotten. Or more like he'd hoped he'd forgotten. The answers there were going to be a bit harder to find.

Never mind, never worry. This was the sort of change that happened to everyone, wasn't it? Just another part of getting old. And what did he have to hide, to be worried about, to be ashamed of? He was sure that if he walked around the shop on a Saturday afternoon – he laughed even at the thought of it – and asked the boys if the same sort of thing happened to them they would have their own stories to tell. About voices and that. Wouldn't they? Wouldn't they?

Go on. G'on.

It started off as a mumble, like a half-whispered prayer after confession.

Go on.

That one was louder. A bit more excited. His eyes moved just slightly to his left. It didn't do to make too much eye contact in a place like this. Personal space was important. What was yours you kept and that was generally respected unless you made it clear that someone was being invited in. Anyway, he didn't know this fella, had never seen him before. He looked thirty, maybe forty at a push, who knew these days when the uniform until you were getting a pension seemed to be tracksuit bottoms, a football shirt, and trainers.

Only then did you start to wear proper trousers.

Go on, the three dog.

It was impossible to ignore this now. Noise levels rarely got above the sudden outburst of swearing at some bad result or other but then reverted quickly to a low drone. The closest thing to it he had heard was the barely audible murmur of bored resignation in the dole office down the town.

As the greyhounds on the screen in front of them hurtled around the second last bend his companion – for that was what he was now as they united in this 30-second vigil – was getting ever more excited. His fingers tightened on the blue betting docket he was holding in his right hand like a modern-day relic.

He looked up at the screen himself, almost begrudgingly but unable to ignore the mini-drama that was unfolding beside him. The 1.59 from Walthamstow, it read in the top right corner. Walthamstow? Where the fuck was Walthamstow? Was that the soap his mother used to sit in front as part of that pathetic nursing home line-up? What was that called? It wasn't Walthamstow, but he was sure it was somewhere in London. Anyway, it would come to him.

The screen to the left of the race had the betting on it. The 3 dog was the 7/4 second favourite, having opened at 2s so there must have been a bit of money for it. It was in a red jacket and the favourite, the 5 dog was in blue. Red and blue. It was such an impersonal business they didn't even bother giving them names anymore, or at least not names that anyone used. He was sure they got called by their names when they were at home or getting fed. You couldn't call a dog for his dinner or for a walk by going, Come on 3 dog. Come on 3 dog, food's up, could you?

The favourite had been marked up at the start at 5/4 and had stayed steady at that. A good strong favourite was always a good thing because it kept the rest of the market honest and forced the bookies to go looking for the punters. They were picking up pace now as they got to the last bend. Five, two and then three, went the vaguely disinterested and disengaged commentary from the speaker in the far corner of the shop – and who could blame him. What sort of self-respecting commentator, what sort of self-respecting human being, got excited about something as drab and worthless as this, a dog race from Walthamstow?

Still. Something kept dragging his attention towards the screen. Curiosity, maybe. He stared vacantly, his head tilted slightly upwards. Eastenders, that was what she'd watched in the home. Not Walthamstow. He knew he'd get it in the end. He usually did. Usually, but not always these days. The 3 dog was making ground the whole way up the straight but it looked like he'd left a bit too much to do.

The whisper beside him had by now become a roar.

Go on, you fucker. Go on, the 3 dog. Come on!

The dogs flashed across the line in a multi-coloured whirl. A few seconds of silence was followed by the calling of the result. He didn't think that the 3 dog had got up on the line but he couldn't be sure. Wouldn't bet on it, ha ha.

5 beats 3 with 4 in third.

Bastard, fucking dirty bastard.

With a theatrical flourish, totally out of keeping with the banality of everything else going on around them, the greyhound man who had been standing beside him flicked his docket with the first finger of his right hand into the air. It sailed gracefully across the dead space of the shop before landing beside all its other fallen blue comrades on the floor. Five seconds later, having gathered himself up, the greyhound man was out the door, his day's work seemingly done. A lot of excitement and fuss about a nothing dog race from Walthamstow. There didn't seem much reason to get so worked up.

Eventually B's curiosity got the better of him. Having watched the airborne descent of the beaten docket he'd fixed its position on the floor. It was still lying where it had fallen. After a surreptitious dart around to make sure no-one was looking, he bent over, fumbling at the laces in his left shoe with his right hand to make it look like he had, after all, a legitimate purpose for his sudden, otherwise unexplained change of position. He shot his left hand out to get the docket. With the same economy of movement he was back upright again. Another furtive look confirmed that he hadn't been seen, or at least if he had been seen it wasn't by anyone who really cared. Mission accomplished.

By now he was unaccountably pleased with himself. It's the small things after all that can bring you joy, he thought. And even as he was thinking that he wasn't really sure what he had meant. Something he had read or heard on the radio which had stuck. More of the same old rubbish.

Unfolding the fingers of his left hand to uncover the secreted piece of paper, he moved his right hand over to uncrumple the docket. Uncrumple, was that a word? He didn't know, but it was what he was doing anyway. Continuing on the furtive theme, he stole a quick glance down but couldn't make out the scrawl straight away. Closing his hand again he cursed the standard of modern education system that had all these children coming out of school not able to write properly. What did they do all day? PE? Drawing? It wasn't proper learning anyway, not the sort he had got. A total disgrace.

This was going to take longer than he had first thought. 2.04….W. W? W? Walthamstow, you eejit. 3 dog…£20… Was that a 5 or a 2? A 5, definitely. £50 win. 50 quid? 50 fucking quid? On a dog? That was a week's brew money, a couple of weeks' food shopping, a lot of pints and smokes. And this guy had blown it on a dog, a glorified racing rat. More money than sense, some people. Or just no sense, never mind the money part. What a waste, what a shocking waste. And on a dog too. A dog. He felt sick and annoyed at the same time.

Right that's enough. Enough of this. Enough sickness and annoyance. Enough. B looked around to see who was talking to him, where the voice was coming from. No-one there. Get on with it. Enough. Enough. B moved his hand slowly upwards, first so that it came to rest lightly on his cheek, then carefully towards his lips as if he was comforting a child. There, at the tips of his fingers, he could feel words being made noiselessly, rapidly but without sound. A machine-gun mouth with a silencer attached. There it went again. Quit that stupid talking to yourself. And again. What was this all about?

He shuffled across the floor towards the racing pages tacked to the wall in front of him dragging the toes of his shoes as he walked in that way that used to drive his father mad when he was going out the front door to school. You'll wear those shoes down to the leather walking like that and they have to do you until June, make no mistake about that or you'll be heading to school barefoot. Catch a grip of yourself.

Where had that come from? He hadn't thought about that in years. Who knows?

Today's first puzzle to be figured out was the two o'clock at Cheltenham. This was safer territory, no chance of the voices drowning him out here. B had already had a look at the card in the Irish News this morning after his breakfast. He had made a mental note of a few that he liked but hadn't got too involved. There was something not right, almost disloyal, to think about making the hard decisions about where his money was going to go at home in his kitchen. The proper place, the only place, for that was here in the shop. Everything in its place and a place for everything.

What time was it? Just gone ten to. Plenty of time yet, plenty of time to get this one sorted out. Now, let's see. Through sheer force of habit he looked first down right hand side of the card at the list of jockeys, scanning them for the one name – AP McCoy. The master. Wouldn't have a bad word said about him. This time he was riding one of David Pipe's, Sainte Kadette it was called. Kadette? He hadn't heard that name in a long time. Where did it come from? Wasn't it a car from the 1970s or something? Kadette. He was sure it was.

Reading the line from right to left – just like the Chinese did, some wise guy had told him – B processed the information it contained like a seasoned, punting computer. Carrying 10-13 and so getting seven pounds from the top-weight, winner of his last two starts. It all looked fairly good. What else was there to know? Five others in the race had won their last start as well. That made puzzling this one out a little bit harder. Ruby Walsh had a ride on one of Crowley's that she had sent over from Ireland. They weren't travelling just for the fun of it, went the presumed logic.

What was the betting? The first show was up on the big screen in the bank between the two front doors. McCoy's was the favourite, 2/1, and they were making Franchoek for Alan King the second favourite at 11/4. Decisions, decisions. Well weighted and with McCoy on board, it was all pointing only one way.

B reached into his trouser pocket for the pen he always carried with him on betting shop expeditions. A cheap black thing, but it did the job. The shop had their own small blue biros, but you could never find one just when you needed it and they always seemed to have run out. There were clear plastic biros tied on strings on the betting benches but more often than not they had no ink left or some comedian had broken the nib. You would think the boss man would check them when he was opening up in the morning. Wouldn't you?

Without needing to look, he thrust his right hand upward, as a child would answer a question in class, towards the Perspex holder screwed to the wall for a betting slip. With his pen in one hand and using the other to hold the blue piece of paper in place, B began to write.

SIX

He was starting to feel dead now. Wasn't that a strange thing to say, a stranger way to be? Alive and thinking and feeling and at the same time pretending to be the opposite. The living dead. And why? Because if they came back and found him, found a witness, they'd kill him. No question about that.

Come back? Maybe they've never left, he hadn't thought about that. Maybe they were still hunting around the area for their witness, for their prey. And if they found him, he would be killed. Nothing surer. Dead cert, as the boys in work used to say as they selected their in-vain winners from the morning racing pages. Why was he thinking like this? They usually got the horses wrong but this was one dead cert they could be sure of.

What sort of dead body would he make? Stop this, stop this now. That depended on how they decided to kill him. A bullet to the side of the head shouldn't make that much mess and they'd be able to patch him up alright for a wake. But if they chose to give him a beating as a taster, a precursor to what was to follow, well then it could be very different. If they chose to show their authority and mark out their territory as so many cuts, bruises and fractures on the map of his body he could finish up a terrible mess. Why was he thinking like this?

With so many beatings, so many killings going on another kind of coded language had developed. Another one to join the lexicon. The rituals which surrounded the bringing home of a murdered body and the preparations for the funeral which would follow now had a new question added to them.

Is the coffin going to be open?

Open was good, closed was bad. Open was good because it denoted and communicated a definite absence of any significant suffering, or at least anything terrible to the face that was visible and could not be concealed, patched up by an undertaker's artistry.

But a closed coffin carried with it its own awful subtext. It was unspoken but that was only because the brutality of the words was better in than out. What a fucking strange thing to find yourself wishing for – an open coffin. What had the fucking world, this fucking world come to?

When had he first seen a dead body? He remembered the word they used above everything else. Corpse. This strange, impersonal otherworldly word that he had never heard before. He didn't know the word, didn't recognise it, but he knew it couldn't be good.

Was he eight? Maybe nine. His granda had been sick. Another strange word – stroke – was mumbled quietly between the adults gathered in their kitchen. The way it was used was a clear indication that he wasn't supposed to hear it but it didn't matter because he didn't know what it meant anyway. He knew what it looked and sounded like though, this stroke. After the first one his granda's speech went completely. All that replaced the words were grunts, most of them plaintive and questioning, some of them angry. Bit by small bit he got it back and inched and crawled his way out of those days of dumbed frustration. Eventually he could at least make himself understood.

But just when he'd pushed his boulder to the top of the hill, it suddenly rolled back on top of him and in a matter of seconds crumpled him completely. This time there was no going back. His granda was 57.

That's a big age, he'd told one of the boys from the house next door with exaggerated mock bravado as if to show he knew what he was talking about. He knew nothing.

Do you think? Martin said. I suppose it's ancient alright. Martin's older brother, Terry, came out to where they were sitting on the steps that led up from the street to his granda's house. A shiny, new metal hand rail ran down from just outside the front door to the bottom of the flight of concrete steps below. After a lot of pushing and fighting the social services people had agreed to put it in to help granda get up and down the stairs. He wouldn't get much use out of it now.

They're looking for you inside, Terry said after a long silence.

B picked up a stone from underneath his black plimsoll and skidded it across the street. If they'd been at the beach it might have skipped three or four times. Here, it just clattered to a halt.

I'm not going in.

Why not?

Don't want to. What's it to you anyway?

You'll have to. They're waiting for you. It's your granda.

I know that, but I'm not going in.

It's just a body, a corpse.

That word again.

I'm not scared of it, of him.

Nobody said you were.

He was getting upset now. But he knew that, like the last forkful of dinner, this was something he had to do, to get through.

Are there many in there now? His eyes were still on the road in front of him.

Not many at the minute. It's quiet but it'll get busier when word gets around and people get home from work.

Would you come in with me?

Aye. No problem.

Would you come in with me? Would you stay with me? Who'll come in with me? Who'll stay with me?

There were fewer cars coming past now. Most people would be home from work now and the streets would be denuded accordingly. Until morning at least. If you had no good reason for being out, then there was no point looking for one. Life was safer that way.

How long had he been here now? How many times would he ask himself that fucking question? For the first time since he'd finished up like this – stock-still and hiding – he was thinking about getting up and getting away. That has to be progress, he thought to himself. That has to be clutching at straws, he thought to himself.

One thing was for sure, he couldn't lie here forever. Soon there would be other people, some looking and searching. Maybe they were already gathered behind some security barrier waiting to do just that but had been told they had to wait until it was safe. Get the bomb disposal boys in.

Who would be there? The police? The army? Almost certainly. Maybe a crowd of onlookers as well, the kind of people who had to get out of their houses when there was any prospect of a really good bad-news story. Perhaps his parents as well, drawn there by different imperatives.

> My son hasn't come home. He's usually regular as clockwork. We think it might be him.
>
> Alright love. When we know something you will.

Ma. Da. Over here.

Had he shouted out the words or just imagined them? The terrible urge to roar for attention was suffocating.

> It's alright, ma, I'm fine. I'm lying hiding over here. Over here.

But he swallowed the half-formed and desperate words whole.

The decision had been made. He had to move now. Or he couldn't stay here. Two ways of getting to the same outcome. He had to take his chance, hope that they had gone and get himself as far as away from here as he could. Ronnie Biggs had gone to Brazil. That would be far enough. Slowly, so slowly that anyone not paying full attention would not even have noticed, he moved his left hand tentatively along the ground, like a young bird about to jump out of the nest for the first time. Slowly, slowly. But he could feel nothing only stones, sand and gravel.

His eyes were open now, exaggeratedly so as he focussed on the street light high overhead, just like that wee guy in his class with the eye-patch used to struggle to figure out what was on the blackboard. The light would be his guide, his North Star. But before he could go anywhere he had to be sure of his bearings and his surroundings. Where was the escape route? You stupid bastard, thinking like one of those guys in a Saturday afternoon prisoner of war film. Stupid, stupid bastard.

Pulling one foot along the ground towards himself, and then the other, he drew his knees towards his chest. At the same time his backside and lower back lifted a little off the ground involuntarily. With one movement, one bound, he could be up and away. Run, run. But he still had to be certain of what was around him. Tilting his head to the right he strained hard to focus but could see nothing in the darkness. After a few seconds of readjustment he could just make out the murky outline of the fence he had jumped and scrambled over. Intermittent chinks and shafts of light were struggling through the slats in the fence from the street beyond.

All life that mattered to him at this minute was on the other side of this fence. Inching his right hand away from his side, he groped for an opening. First one finger, then another and then his whole hand was in one of the gaps. Like an amusement arcade grabber he opened and closed his hand, right and left. Nothing.

Just a bit further. Just a bit further. He sidled his entire body to the right so that now his face was up tight against the fence. The creosote was strong and tarry. Don't sneeze, whatever you do, don't sneeze. His wrist and the lower part of his right arm were now through the fence as well. Grasping and groping for some sort of sign.

As he completed another opening and closing of his fist, he felt something. It was a coat or a jacket, heavy fabric anyway. He pushed on a little bit more. Then his hand could go no further. There was something in the way. Pushing again, this time a little more forcefully, he came up against something harder, something more solid. This time there was no mistaking, no more uncertainty. The body on the other side of the fence didn't move.

SEVEN

It was the shake he noticed first. He couldn't take his eyes off it. A tremor, that was the proper name for it, but the only way he could describe it to someone who hadn't seen anything like it before was a shake. It was a shake because it shook and there was nothing anybody could do about it.

The man at the front of queue at the Bet window was barely five feet tall. He was in his 70s. Maybe 80 now. Shorty, he would have got at school, but that was a long time ago. His right hand, his shaking hand, gripped on to a walking stick which on a normal sized man would have been up to his hip but for him was halfway up his stomach. Most of the stick was chrome, or probably imitation chrome, a bit like an elongated kitchen tap. At the top was a dimpled, blue plastic handle and at the bottom a grey rubber stopper. Probably to stop him making too much of a racket out on the street. Or in the aisle of a chapel. The stick looked like the sort you would have got from the NHS during the 1980s. Cheap and nasty. Maybe he'd had it since then. Maybe they were just down to the last few at the hospital or the old people's home and this was all there was when he went looking.

Maybe. Still, he was able to hold on tight to it, like a boy at primary school with laboured-over homework.

The woman at the window was ready for him now. Not that you could really tell the difference, what with her empty eyes and bored movements. That was what this sort of job could do to you, if you let it. With a practised, well-honed move he leant on the counter with his left hand and tilted the stick just a little so it could rest against his hip. That freed his right hand, his shaking hand, to go into his trouser pocket. Then there was a rattle of coins – coppers for sure, you could tell by the sound – which he plopped down on the Formica in front of him looking pleased with himself and his effort.

One, then another, escaped and rolled along the counter before falling silently on to the paper-messed floor. The woman at the tills rolled her eyes, code to anyone watching that she'd seen all this before. Nobody else moved. After a few seconds B could bear it no longer. With one stride he was on top of the errant money.

Thanks, young fella, thanks a million.

Young fella, he liked that. It didn't take much, mind you. Why wasn't there more of that about? Just casual, not-thought-about compliments. Then again, silly, ageing men didn't need much to make them feel better about themselves.

The man was starting to count now and at the same time was trying to direct operations.

One pound forecast on the three and six dog, love, in the next. Could you write the docket for me? The hand's playing up, there's a good girl.

He held up his shaking hand in front of her, as if to emphasise his point. That way she couldn't refuse him. It dangled horribly and lifelessly before she reached wearily to the side of her seat for a stubbed pencil. He'd made his point.

The money was pushed forward in four irregular piles.

How much is there? she grumbled at him.

A pound. Isn't that the bet you wrote out for me?

She didn't look up.

96, 97, 98, 99, 100. You've too much, she half-grunted through the slits in the glass, as if telling off a badly-behaved child, emptying one 2p and a penny out on to the counter.

I thought it was right. It's not like you people to be giving me anything back.

The attempt at a joke fell flat. Using an unruly ragged nail on his right hand the man lifted the money up, first the two and then the one. Tightening the muscles at the top of his arm, just where it met his shoulder, he summoned one last effort to control the shake and got the coins into the slot at the top of a Guide Dogs charity box which was chained to the rail that supported the Bet window's Perspex sheet.

There's my good deed done for the day. One step closer to that place in heaven.

Hope it brings you a bit of luck, B said.

The words were out before he'd even made up his mind to say them. What had happened there? Going soft he was, going soft in his old age.

Still, take it where you can get it. This was the most civilised conversation he'd had in years, at least with someone he didn't know. Good manners are easy carried, they'd taught him that at school. Nobody had thought to tell this shower of fuckers in here, had they? It made him feel strange, a bit uneasy, this sudden outbreak of civility. Just when he least expected it as well. Even stranger was the way he had matched it, seen it and raised it with some more kind words. What was that all about? It might only have been getting a few coppers off the floor for a near-cripple, but it was as much as he'd done for anyone in a long time. Anyone other than himself. And he hadn't even been asked, that was the strange thing. Maybe that was what would make all the difference, having someone to care about, to be nice to, civil to. That's what would help him change. Not love, not being in love, or any of that rubbish. Just an occasional act of kindness. A shaft of light in the clearing. He was surprised how it made him feel. Nearly good about himself, nearly but not quite.

His old, new friend was making painfully slow progress down the middle of the shop. For all the strangeness of his physical appearance and his obvious decrepitude, he might as well have been invisible for all the attention anyone paid him. Men moving between the bank of screens and the betting windows breezed past him, close enough to brush against his jacket but so far away that they never once made eye contact. Not one of them. The man who wasn't there, alone in this crowd of maleness and lonely self-absorption. B almost felt sorry for him now, the sad old bastard. But then he did a double-take, took a step back. Who gives a fuck about me in here? About me? No point in me wasting my time on any of them the way they treat me, not even this poor, old guy. Every man for himself. It's easier that way. No one to be let down by. Not secrets to keep, or confidences to be broken. Say nothing. Watch my lips. I'm saying nothing.

Anyway, shake yourself. You're next. Step right up for the bet that will change your life. What was it they talked about? A life-changing sum of money. Half of that would do. Any win would be enough at the minute. Something is an improvement on nothing.

There was only one seat left at the end of the row in front of the screens. B sat down, fingering his newly-acquired betting slip like a relic or a rosary. He stated vacantly ahead. Lights are on, nobody at home. Same old routine. Waiting.

EIGHT

B had to hear the creak of the third stair from the top before he could be sure who was going down the stairs first. Years of getting up long before everyone else had made his mother adept at the most noiseless of movements as she got first herself and then the house ready before going out to one of her long procession of cleaning jobs. She knew the potential peril of that step from the bitter experience of it waking up one of the babies and then fighting a long battle to get him settled so she wouldn't be late. Now, all these years later, her slippered feet barely touched the staircase on the way down. Feather-light.

But it was still enough of a clue for B who was lying in his bed still awake and staring vacantly at the ceiling, listening, listening. It was as if his ears had now become so finely tuned that his hearing had supplanted all of his other senses. Just like that Helen Keller story they'd read at school.

Click. Then, scrape. That was the back door being opened, followed immediately by the draught excluder dragging along the kitchen floor. Cluck, clonk, clutter. Cluck, clonk, clutter. That was his mother filling the coal bucket from the bunker which was buttressed up against the wall to the right of the back gate. She walked back in more slowly, and with slightly heavier steps than when she had gone out because of the weight of the bucket. This hard life isn't getting any easier. He couldn't hear her think – he wasn't that good – but that was what was going through her head. She had said it enough times in that barely-spoken voice parents used to get their point across but without making too much of a fuss. Or so they thought. Don't mind me, I'm only giving off. The English had a posh way of saying the same thing – letting off steam. But his mother never let off steam. She just complained, quietly.

This was home. This was home. His bed. His house. His noises. After that he wasn't sure of anything. He shut his eyes and opened them only when he felt a pushing down of the blankets somewhere near the bottom of the bed. He recognised the sensation, registered the memory. That feeling of being cocooned in your bed by the physical presence of someone sitting on it to read you a story or to tell a tall tale. Move a wee bit, please. My feet are all scrunched up.

This was different though. The illusion was broken by his father's voice.

> Where were you until all hours? We waited up as long as we could and then it was as much as I could do to stop you ma from going next door to use their phone and get the police. She was worried half to death.

> Sorry. Nowhere, I was nowhere. Just around and about. We went out after work and one thing led to another and we finished up in a late night place in town. Then it took ages to get a taxi back up the road again.

> Jesus, are you mad or what? Out and about in the streets with all sorts going on. You're going to get yourself killed. You never know what could have happened to you. Don't be at it again if you want to keep your backside under this roof.

The tone in which that barely-concealed threat was delivered was a clear indication that no answer was expected and that the conversation was at an end. His father got up and walked purposefully out the door. He had said his piece. Unlike the slippery gentleness of his mother just before, his boots struck the thin lino and the wooden boards underneath with loud authority. His boots. His floor. His house.

It hadn't crossed B's mind for a single second that he should tell his father the truth or anything like that. After that, he must have dozed off again. He opened and closed his eyes, then repeated the sequence once, twice, three times as if trying to blink some reality into his half-awake self. His room was at the same time familiar and terrifying. This was his bed, his world, but he wasn't even sure how he had got here. Here and not-here at the same time.

To his right, the dishwater-scum-yellow of the street light just outside the window was leaking through the gap in the curtains. He always left them open like that. Not because he was afraid of the dark or anything like that. Nothing like that.

> Why do you do that? his mother would ask him with a laugh. A big boy like you.
>
> Get away out of it and leave me alone. It's just what I like.

What he couldn't explain was why. He liked lying there, just awake, with that lit possibility of the world outside and all it had to offer. It was stupid really. But closing the curtains would remove all that possibility and limit him hopelessly. It didn't make him feel safer. It just made him feel more alive. Or was it less dead?

B reached across, just like he had done the night before, only this time with his right hand. The table on that side of the bed was cold to his touch and empty, except for the old tick-tock alarm clock. It hadn't gone off yet. Or maybe he hadn't set it. Either way it didn't matter, because he wasn't going in today. That much was certain. He just couldn't. Not after all of this.

Part of him wanted to stretch out his left arm too, but he kept it tight underneath the blankets as if he was afraid of what it might feel. But that was stupid, wasn't it? There was nothing there. Of course, there was nothing there. How could there be? Maybe there never had been anything. It had been a dream. Another stupid fucking dream.

Tom at work fancied himself as a bit of an expert at figuring out what dreams meant and he used to torture them all at break-times looking for raw material.

> All your teeth were falling out, is that what you said? Let me think. Yeah, that's a sign you're going to inherit a lot of money some time very soon.
>
> What a load of shite, someone piped up from the back in between a bite out of his fishpaste sandwich and a slurp from his enormous mug of tea. The only explanation you can ever give about people's dreams is that it means they're going to get a load of money.
>
> That's right, said someone else. It's all the same rubbish all the time.

A workplace consensus was emerging and Tom was in trouble. B just listened. He knew his place. On the defensive now, Tom did his best.

> That's not true and you know it. Didn't one of you have one where you were being chased through a forest or up the Cavehill or something and I knew it meant that somebody close to you was going to die?
>
> Aye, my granny. But that was six months later.

The laughter was louder this time. Proper, deep, throaty laughs. And that's how Tom got his nickname. Bad Dreams. When he walked through the workshop someone was guaranteed to shout out. Here comes Bad Dreams. That means there must be money, or something like that, on the way.

Just wait until he heard this one, although it was pretty easy to see where it would fit in. Something bad on the way. Something bad had already happened. It's not my fault, B whispered to himself, his palm over his mouth so he could swallow the words as soon as they were out. It's not my fault.

His were the third pair of feet on the stairs that morning as he inched his way down in his sock soles, his boots held by their tongues in his right hand. He had dressed quickly in yesterday's clothes but he couldn't find his coat. Where was his coat? Had he come home without his coat? Where had he left it? Who was going to find it? The door into the kitchen was closed. He could just make out the drone of the radio on the dresser just on the other side of it. His da's work coat was still hanging over the bottom of the stairs. After snibbing the lock and slipping noiselessly out the front door, he started to walk. It was all he could find in himself to do. He had to walk. He had to walk.

It had now been an hour, give or take, since he'd left the house. He had come down the hill from the house and just kept on going into town. Because he had no bag no-one bothered with him at the biggest of the security checks in the middle of town and he had walked straight through. He paid little attention to what was going on around him. Walking was enough for now, just keep going. Random thoughts came and went. He was hungry. How long was it since he had eaten? Last night anyway, and then no breakfast this morning. He was cold. Where was his coat? Something had happened to it. What?

This part of town – around the university – wasn't really somewhere he knew. Somebody belonging to his mother – her cousin maybe – used to live around here. He worked as a cleaner at the university. Or was it a porter? Was there a difference? They used to come up here on a Sunday to visit him. Now and again, if he was in a good mood, he'd buy them a poke of ice cream in the park. He called it The Gardens but it was really just a park. Where was that? Somewhere up this way. Some ice-cream would be nice. And a flake.

A stooped man in a blue woollen work jacket and green overalls was fiddling with the lock on the gate. Days and weeks and months of doing the same thing every morning had bent his back into that position. He looked like he couldn't stand up straight even if he wanted to.

This frigging thing. We have to lock up at night because

this is where they all come when they're hiding from the peelers. And then I can never get the lock to take in the morning.

The park man seemed to be talking to himself. Then he looked up.

On the go in good time this morning, son? Up early to see what's what. Is that what it is?

B didn't answer. He looked around. This was definitely the park they'd come to before. But it didn't seem as alive as it had been then. It just looked different. Everything was still asleep, even the plants, dormant. It had always been summer before. All the trees and flowers were dressed then. Now he felt like he'd walked in on them before they'd had a chance to get their clothes on. He felt embarrassed for them. Wasn't that stupid?

The park man walked slowly ahead of him, as if he was being paid by the step. The path wound around to the right towards a denuded, circular flower bed. He stopped there, pulled a packet of smokes out of his right hand trouser pocket, picked one and lit it affectionately with a match fished out his jacket pocket. The first puff of smoke burnt a trail through the frost of the morning air. Like aeroplane vapour. The lock of the latticed door of the Palm House opened much more easily. A swirl of warm air escaped, then disappeared as he went inside.

The front of the museum was like nothing he'd ever seen. They – his ma and her cousin – had definitely never come up this far, up towards the main road. The place where the ice-cream man used to be was close enough, just behind the three big trees that stood guard outside but they had never come past there.

The museum was just strange. All stone and cement, no bricks at all. All straight lines and angles. Where was the roof? Where were the gutters? There was something about it that frightened him. It was off-putting, like a big library or something. Not somewhere he was ever going to rush into. The longer he looked at it, the more he noticed. The way balconies and ledges seemed to hang in mid-air over the front door, looking like they had somewhere important to go but hadn't made up their mind yet. His eyes were drawn all over the place, up and down and from side to side and he struggled to take in all the detail.

Maybe that's what he found strangely upsetting about it, this way it was making him feel. The curves in the Palm House were easier to take in, a bit like looking at a white, glass chapel. It was a place designed to make you feel calm and better about yourself. But it seemed to him that the whole point of this new museum was to make you feel the exact opposite. Not settled, asking questions, almost unhappy. Maybe that was the idea, the big plan.

If it was, B didn't get it. The narrow streets around his way were all bricks, windows and slates, nothing more and nothing less. But you could live them, feel safe in them. Imagine trying to live here. Maybe they hadn't been able to get enough bricks for a building this size and had to use to concrete instead? But that was stupid, there was a brick works place still going just up the road. Or maybe it was too dear to do it that way. At least that would be an excuse.

He pushed at the revolving door in the middle of the museum's front. It didn't budge. A key turned on the other side of the fixed door beside it with a big sign marked Exit in the middle of it.

> Come on in, son, you're the first of the day. No prize for that though.

Once inside, B walked up the stairs on the left beside the lift. One flight, then two, three and four. Even when he was going nowhere but up, one step then the next, it felt good to be moving, to be getting away. Better than sitting still. Or lying there. He kept climbing, faster and faster now, relishing the breathlessness and sense of otherness it brought. The sense of being outside himself looking in was one he loved.

NINE

I like to go down about half four, quarter to five, just when the light is starting to go. That's the best time.

B looked to his right to see where the voice was coming from. It was the old man with the stick from before.

It takes me a while to get there, with the stick and that, but it's worth it. If you keep going over the bridge, down beside where the leisure centre used to be and where they have those new flats looking over the river, that's the best place. The best view. I hear there's maybe 30,000 of them now, starlings resting here for the winter. God bless their wit. Are they going north or south? Do you know? No matter, they're here anyway enjoying the Belfast winter. They sleep under the bridge you know, all of them. I heard something on the radio that there are five million of them in Rome, five million, and the smell is something terrible. Lucky we miss that with them away under the bridge. But you have to be there before they go in for the night. You should see it.

They put on some show swooping up and down over the bridge. Like a floating cloak, somebody beside me said the other night. I thought that was good. A floating cloak. Like a priest. For me it's like a big cloud of dust, black moving dust. Every now and then one of the breaks away but he doesn't stay outside the group for too long. Then he's back and they're away again. It really is so beautiful. Have you been down? Do you know why they do it? To show off, or for exercise? I don't know. It's definitely worth seeing though, better than anything on the TV anyway. What day is it today? Saturday, isn't it? I was down last Thursday night, just for twenty minutes or so before it got too cold. I was looking up at the swirl of all those birds and I started crying. Crying! Can you believe that? Especially at my age. I was looking up at the way the whole lot of them were moving around and it reminded me of my son blowing bubbles. Jesus, that must be forty years ago. He'd been on at me for ages to get him the stuff. You know the way they can keep going on about something. So, one night on the way home from work I stopped off at the paper shop and bought him a tube of that bubbles stuff, you know with the stick with a circle at the end stuck on to the lid. That's what you blow through. He was only delighted. I can see him now standing in the middle of our back kitchen blowing them out up and towards the light bulb. Look, Daddy, it's a rainbow of bubbles. At the start he was blowing too hard and the bubbles were no sooner out than they'd pop. But he got the hang of it soon enough, blowing more slowly so that the bubbles had to force themselves out through the circle. That made them go into funny shapes, not really circles, more like squashed circles, bent in at the sides. Do you know what I mean? That's what those starlings look like when they're flying up there and really at themselves. He had great fun, the young fella, but then his sister wanted a go and between them they managed to knock the container on to the ground. Just an accident, like, but he was so upset. He got down on his hands and knees and was trying to scoop and push the liquid back into the container. It's not fair, he kept saying over and over, looking up at me and then back to the floor. They were so beautiful, he said. And then he started to really cry.

Where's your son now? B asked, again almost despite himself.

He died. He died.

B crumpled himself down into one of the red plastic bucket seats. One of the unspoken rules of this place, his place, was nothing personal, nothing that might give any part of you away. What you have you hold. Anything else just wasn't up for discussion. That was it. He slipped effortlessly into default mode. This was a shut-down situation because no matter what his guard could never come down. You could never be sure what might tumble out otherwise.

What do you make of this next one, the Paddy Power Chase? Real bastards these handicaps, the best horses get too much weight and donkeys at the bottom get far closer than they ever should. Have you had a look? There's two who are out of the handicap down near the bottom, and they're dragging everyone else down with them. McCoy's on one of Jonjo's – Rob Hall. I think I saw his last one. Third he was, but McCoy wasn't too hard on him as far as I could see. The pick of them, though, is L'Antartique. The boys were talking all about him on Channel 4 this morning. Not carrying too much compared to the top three or four and Graham Lee's a decent pilot. Those two in a reverse forecast, what do you think?

The old man's rheumy, falling-down eyes stared straight ahead. His voice had dropped almost to a whisper. The mumbled, prayer-like tone was all but lost in the barrage of horse and greyhound commentaries from the screens in front of them.

> It was the night before Halloween. I was just in from work, about half five it was, and I met him at the front door. He was said he was going out to play for a while. He was only eleven. No fireworks, I remember saying to him, they could put your eye out those things if you don't watch. Stay safe. I don't know if he looked at me or not. I was hanging my coat over the bottom of the stairs. Daddy, you don't have to worry about things like that. He walked up the street. The last thing I saw was him pulling up the hood of his anorak, like he was protecting himself from the cold. It had started to rain a bit heavier. I remember thinking it was the first time I'd ever seen him do that, think about how to look after himself without being told by either of us. At last, I said to myself, he's getting a bit of sense after all these years.

He sucked in a mouthful of air, some fuel for the journey.

> I was out in the back kitchen then I heard the wife go to answer the front door. It wasn't an ordinary knock. You'd better come up quick to the new road. Something's happened. When we got up there, it was so quiet. No traffic at all. That was the first strange thing. There were queues of car, lorries and a bus or two building up in both directions. Somewhere near the back of the one heading towards town I could hear a horn being beeped. It was one of those bad-tempered horn sounds, not the sort you would make to warn someone to get out of the way. I was cross at him for that. Don't ask me why. Someone's always got something more important to do than you, haven't they?

59

B's attention strayed for a second to the screen showing the Cheltenham race. He felt immediately guilty, like he'd interrupted a priest in a confession box, but he couldn't help himself. Force of habit. There was some sort of hold-up at the start of the race. They couldn't hear what was going on. The old man was looking at it too, but his stare was fixed and empty.

Where had he seen that look before? It was how he imagined a dead man might look, not immediately after he had died but once the body had come to terms with what had happened. The immediate terror replaced with something slightly more distant, maybe more at peace. How a dead man might look.

He thought he had seen it in the living as well. There were two women, two sisters, who, once a week, would make their way slowly back up from the market, over the bridge and up the hill towards the convent. Their legs were straight but their backs were doubled over from the waist up. Walking right angles. They moved in sequence and in line like footballers in a pre-match parade. Their ruffled blouses were identical but their cardigans were subtly different shades of blue. He used to wonder if that was an accident or on purpose. Had one faded in the sun or been washed more than the other? He didn't think they could ever have meant to appear different. Laden down with plastic bags of shopping, two in each hand to balance, they looked up only to check for traffic as they crossed the road opposite the betting shop. That's when he had seen their faces.

B felt guilty for the break in the story, but he didn't know why. He had an uneasy feeling that they wouldn't be able to go back now, that the journey back had been broken and couldn't be resumed. But why was he guilty? That didn't make sense, did it? It wasn't his fault. None of all of this was his fault, was it? Was it? The old man started again.

> I saw a lorry stopped in the middle of the road. It seemed so out of place there. Not moving when it should be going somewhere, delivering something, getting the driver home. I don't know. It was big thing. I felt so

small looking up at it. It looked like it was for moving furniture, you know the sort of thing I'm talking about. That's where the crowd was gathered. And my boy was underneath the front wheel. Still there, he was. All I could see were his feet sticking out. All I could think about was that his mother would be cross with him for not changing his school shoes when he got home. He knew he was supposed to do that and put on his old gutties. Otherwise, we wouldn't get the shoes to last much beyond Christmas. They'd been playing this game you see, him and this other wee lad, called Chicken. I'd never heard of that before. Why would I have, I suppose. They'd got hold of an old bit of rope somewhere and went to opposite sides of the road, still holding on to one end of it each. When a lorry was coming you had to hold on as long as you could and the last one to let go was the winner. Then they'd start all over again, keeping score until, I suppose, it was time to go home. The thing was our boy wrapped his end around his wrist to give him a better chance. When the lorry came he wasn't able to let it go, maybe he didn't want to let it go, anyway, it just pulled him under the front wheels. That was it. That was it. After all the bother we'd had round our way since the start of all the trouble, he gets killed like that. What a fucking stupid way to go.

The swear word was like a full stop to the story. The old man checked himself for a second, shocked by the bad language he had used. B could tell it wasn't really his thing.

Sorry about that. I don't usually speak like that. It's just, it's just…

It's alright, I can see why.

Now it was B's turn to stop for a few seconds. That was probably the nicest, kindest thing he had said to anyone in years. What was going on here? He didn't like it. Let's talk about it, old girlfriends used to say to him during the times when he'd go quiet on them. Let's not, he'd eventually bite back, refusing to revisit places he'd long left behind. Nothing good ever came from opening yourself up, letting people know what you knew or had to say. Or what you'd seen or what you remembered. Let's just not.

The old man had gone. Well, not gone, but he wasn't standing with B any more. Was this how it was supposed to finish? He didn't know. The air was now heavy with laughter from the seats in front of the big screens.

> Up Chelsea, someone shouted and snorted out a half-laugh. Up Chelsea.

At first it was impossible to see what it was all about. But he was sure it was the laugh of someone not all there. That was one thing for certain. There was no football on the screen. Never was. The shop didn't have the contract for it, or some other excuse. More like they were too mean to pay the money.

It quickly became obvious who the shouting was aimed at. B had seen this man a few times before. He was always dressed the same, head to toe in Man United gear – tracksuit top and bottoms at this time of year with a bobble hat on top. He had a strange, ugly kind of face, as if his eyes were being permanently squashed up into his forehead by a pencil forced up his nose. A pug dog on long spindly legs. The Chelsea shout came up again. The United man knew it was meant for him but he pretended to stare ever more intently at the results page flickering down from above him. This was taking all his effort not to react but when it started a third time he couldn't keep it in any longer.

> Fuck away off, will you? Do you like the taste of hospital food, because that's what you'll be getting. Do you like hospital food. Do you? Do you?

This produced only more guffaws of laughter.

Do you like hospital food? B thought it was the most idiotic threat he had ever heard in his life.

TEN

When he could go up no further he stood on the landing and got his bearings. On three sides there were imposing, double mahogany doors, each with two thick glass panels in their top half and an ornate, brass handle-plate about two-thirds of the way up. They were pieces of door furniture that screamed solidity and tradition. No messing around up here. To Galleries, an embossed sign on the wall read. To galleries it was then. The first pair of doors he came to were unbelievably heavy to the touch and the sensation of pushing them open was like going into a chapel after Mass had started. He had to push harder than expected to get through.

They swooshed closed behind him and he looked around. There were paintings, big paintings, everywhere he looked, on all four walls. He blinked and tried to take it all in, slightly bewildered by the assault of size and colour, like someone readjusting after moving from the dark into a beam of bright light.

Another sign, much smaller this time, on the wall told him these were 18th Century Paintings of Local Interest. Whatever that meant. He was still struggling with the impact of everything around him.

And he was hungry. How had he forgotten about that? Why hadn't he eaten yet? He would have to get something soon.

The room was dominated by a long, wooden bench that ran its entire length down the middle of the room. It was made from the same solid stuff as the doors. He knew that much. The bench curved slightly in its middle when he sat down. It was made in a way which encouraged you to sit for a while and take everything in. He liked that because it wasn't the same as those hard pews at Mass, the sole purpose of which seemed to be to get you on your knees and keep you there for as long as possible.

On the wall facing him there was a painting which completely filled the space between two lead windows on either side. Running his eyes from one side to the other, from the top to the bottom and then from one corner to the one opposite he drank it all in. He gulped involuntarily, the hurried swallow an indication of the feelings that were washing over him. He had never seen anything like this in his life before.

A few seconds, maybe a minute, passed. He wanted so much to get up, go over and take a closer look but he wasn't sure if he would be allowed. That was stupid, wasn't it? This wasn't school or the chapel but it felt like it. It seemed to him like the sort of place where you needed permission to do almost anything, where there was always someone above you in the pecking order who was most definitely in charge.

After furtive looks, first to one end of the cold room and then to the other, B walked over to the painting. He was up close now, bending over just a little to read the small brass plate at the bottom. Strickland Lowry, attributed to, The Family of Thomas Bateson (1762). It took him a while to digest that and figure out what it meant in relation to the picture in front of him. The first bit was the name of the painter, he knew that much. He didn't know what the second bit meant at all but the last of the words definitely were meant to tell you who these people were. So far so good.

Raising himself back to his full height, he turned around and went back to his place on the bench. Even the words and names were an attack on his senses. Strickland Lowry was not like any name he had ever heard up round their way. Was it two second names, anyway? He smiled. One was probably the first name but he didn't know which. Or maybe he had two first names. It was long enough ago and maybe it was different then. It definitely sounded important, and maybe that was enough. Important enough for a painter anyway. He said the name into himself a few times and smiled again. It was a name just made for a posh voice. Like a newsreader.

The Family of Thomas Bateson. These must be his children. Two girls and three boys. Or at least he thought the three on the right were boys even though they had long, tied-back hair. They looked rich. No, they were rich. The piano and the table and chairs at the back told him that.

What age were they? The girls looked like teenagers, the boys a bit younger. They all looked very serious. Why not, he supposed, it was probably a big thing to get this done, to stand statue-still in your front room and get yourselves painted. He reckoned he would be serious-looking too, best Holy Communion face.

The more he looked, the more he saw. The black dog in the middle looking up at the youngest boy. It was almost blended into the background until you fought to pick it out by finding first one of the eyes, then the other. Probably begging for food. But even with all the people at the front B's eyes kept drifting towards the back of the picture. First to the two paintings on the wall. A painting with more paintings in it. Now that was funny. Were they pictures of Belfast? Maybe. Why else would the painting be here? Were the Batesons from Belfast? He had never heard the name before but they might have been from over in the East. Or the country. There were also black and white pictures of other people, adults, most likely relations and maybe their parents. But why didn't they get into the main painting? That seemed a bit strange. Maybe they were standing at the side, just out of view, looking in and keeping the children and the dog under control.

The circle on wheels at the front was a globe. One of the boys was pointing at it. Was it his and did he want the world to know? Or was he telling everyone that as soon as he could he was getting out of here, out of this .city, out of this painting and off to another world. Where did he want to go? B thought he was pointing towards Africa. He leaned forward, putting his hands on his knees to balance himself, to check that it was. And up in the corner, near the wooden frame, he could just make out Ireland. Little Ireland.

The brother on the other side of the globe was holding something, a compass maybe, in one hand and piece of paper in the other. He looked the most serious of the lot and the one who was most in a hurry to get the whole painting thing over with. B wondered what sort of painting his own family would get done. Well, for a start there would have to be other people, aunts and uncles, in it, in case any of them got offended. His da would hate it as well. He knew that. Can't see the point of this rubbish, he'd say. Besides, we haven't got a wall big enough to put it up on.

He had been alone in the room all this time. Then out of the corner of his eye, he saw a man dressed in what must have been a museum uniform walking towards him.

> Not many stop at this one for some reason, he said.
> I don't like it myself. There's something missing.
> Where's the mother? The mother stands for comfort,
> for someone to love those children. And she's not there.
> That picture's got a big secret it's not telling.

After the warming stale air of the museum, the cold wind caught in the back of his throat as he walked around the path and down towards the Palm House. He had his bearings a little better now. Just over the big flower bed and beyond the hedge was where the man had sold the ice-creams from his van. And just to the left of there was the big bit of grass where they had played football.

At least it was open. He pushed the white, latticed door and immediately found his eyes drawn upwards into the vast, domed roof. It was like a chapel or a cathedral only with glass. There were plants and trees everywhere, seeming to fill every available space. Not the sort he was used to in the parks around their way. These were different. What was the word? Fancy? No, not that. He'd read it somewhere, maybe in a geography book or in the Childcraft encyclopaedia the teacher had kept, venerated, on her desk. Exotic. That was it. Exotic. He rolled the word around in his mouth, enjoying the strange feeling of the x and the t and the c, all together. It was a different kind of word. And a better kind of word.

The walkway went circular in each direction. He turned left. On either side of him as he walked branches and stems and tentacles of weird and wonderful plants brushed against his arms and shoulders. He liked the way they did that, the physical contact. The comfort of it felt reassuring and brought with it a kind of peace. He stopped for a few seconds just to feel the plants on his arms, elbows and shoulders. It was like they were hugging at him. It had been a long time.

A door, still to his left, opened into a bigger, less claustrophobic rectangular room with a passageway that ran right to the far end. The first thing, the only thing, he noticed was the magnificent assault of the heady, perfumey smell that blasted at him as he walked in. It was sweet, but not sickly. There was an acidic, almost unpleasant layer to the smell that seemed designed to keep you just a little on edge. There was pleasure to be given up but it was complicated, not about to reveal itself easily or all at once.

Banked shelves ran down both sides of this cooler room. Well, he assumed there must be shelves because banks of hundreds of pots all containing the same type of flower rose up from the ground to close to eye-level. They were clearly the same but in great swathes of different colours, red and white and purple and blue. Or was that lilac? And each of them ascended delicately out of its pot in a cone-like shape, like mini-Christmas trees only with delicate pearled flowers instead of needles.

B didn't know their name but he knew the smell. In the hall at the front door of his school the caretaker had set up a Nature Table. That made it sound a lot grander than it actually was because for most of the year it was home to a few decaying leaves, some pine cones and a picture showing the lifecycle of a frog. But for a couple of weeks just after the Christmas holidays three innocuous looking brown pots were added to the display. At the start all you could see when you peered in was soil but as the days passed and January turned into February the dirt was forced to the side little by little as the new lives emerged. And on one morning, without anybody noticing that it was just about to happen, the entire new flowers were there. And with that came the smell, the blast of that fresh sweet smell every time the front door opened.

And this was the same smell. But instead of just three there were many tens and hundreds of them. What was their name? B rolled his tongue in his mouth as if trying to move the remembering process along but it was no good. Bulbs. That was all he could come up with. He knew that they must have come from bulbs. Someone had said the flowers came from bulbs that you planted. New life from the dead ground. The miracle of fresh, bright life from the darkness. What had been lying lifeless and silent for a long time could – after the dangerous cold of winter had begun to pass – show its head again once it was safe, once the threat had disappeared with the renewed heat of the sun. He liked that idea. He needed that idea to be true. But what happened next? After a week or two of blousy show, a great display of colour and smell, real life seemed to elbow its way back in and the inexorable process of decay began all over again. What could you do about that?

Back out in the domed middle of the Palm House he looked up at the rising curves of glass and metal. The challenge of it all. How had they been able to do that? How had anyone dreamt that up? Building a roof made of glass seemed brave enough, but how to get it to curve as well. Bendy glass. Now there was a thing. Bendy glass. The words were funny on his tongue, ridiculously absurd to describe the magnitude of what was needed to put together a building like this. Bendy glass. That would be a good one for the lads at tea-break. You were where? Jesus, would you listen to your man with his fancy ideas and his trips up around the university. What's in your lunch box the day – encyclopaedia sandwiches? How was he going to go back to them, back to all of that, after what had happened to him last night? After all that he had seen? Or not seen. How was he going to be able to tell anyone? Tell what though? What had he seen? All he had done was lie there and play dead. Playing dead while life had gone on all around him. Or maybe it was death.

The room on the opposite side was totally different. Hotter and wetter. Drops fell from the ceiling on to B's head as he walked in. He looked to his right at the fogged-up windows. He couldn't work out where all the heat was coming from. Then he noticed the thick, hot-water pipes that ran underneath the length of the windows. There were no sweet-smelling flowers in here. If the other room was light and welcoming, comforting almost, this was a humid and oppressive place. A place to survive in, not to thrive in.

Everything that was growing here seemed other-worldly, like it didn't belong in this grim, gloomy city on the edge of Europe. The shiny-leafed plants and trees pushed and bullied through and around each other as if they were trying to escape, were trying to break through the glass, and get back to where they had come from and where they belonged. Somewhere on the other side of the world, somewhere at least away from here.

It felt like a forced habitat to him. There was nothing natural about this over-heated glass room sitting on the edge of a gloomy, deserted park. He didn't like it, this otherness and he was unsettled by it. But he kept on walking. Down at the end there was a gate which he opened. The path led around behind the central collection of plants and back towards the door where he had come in. There was a high, white-washed wall to the side. Vines snaked up the full height of the wall. They were tied and fixed intermittently with thin, brown twine. Scattered randomly across the vines were lustrous bunches of green and red grapes. It all seemed impossibly glamorous, unreal almost.

B looked furtively around, first left, then right and then behind. There was no-one around. Why would there be, at this time?

Slowly and deliberately he inched his right hand out of his coat pocket and reached tentatively upwards. His thumb and forefinger enveloped a red grape which was on the outside of a bunch of ten, maybe twenty others. Turning his thumb slowly, anti-clockwise, he eased the grape off its stalk with the delicacy of a surgeon. Sure he was going to be caught, he didn't want to make any noise, any sound, in case he might be noticed. What would happen to him then?

By now it was too late. Afraid even to look at it, he closed his eyes and placed the grape on his tongue. He savoured the taste and the juice for a few seconds and then put his hand back in his pocket, hurried along the rest of the path out into the main hall and out the front door of the Palm House. It was the first thing he had eaten all day and he already felt sick to the very pit of his stomach.

ELEVEN

B stood with the rest of the sentry-men at the front door of the betting shop. He, like them, was having a smoke. They didn't speak to one another and if truth be told barely recognised one another's presence. Ritual had brought them together and the connection did not go any deeper than that.

Just across the road B could see some pilgrims about to tread the well-worn penitent path from the pub to the betting shop. Even though there was a pedestrian crossing just down the road, outside the next pub along and opposite the paper shop, these experienced travellers never used it. Instead, they would step off the footpath into the traffic, regardless of whether it was clear to cross or not. Then with an extravagant flourish of the free hand that was not holding a sheaf of scribbled betting slips they would effectively force any car or van in their way to stop and allow them to get to the other side. The forced arresting of the particular vehicle's progress was invariably met with an extravagant thumbs up or a pseudo-grateful nod of the head in the direction of the driver. Once they got halfway across the entire process was then repeated, this time in order to stop the traffic coming in the opposite direction. This well-worn method of road management seemed to be unique to men – only men – trying to get from the pub to the betting shop and then back again. It was not, B thought to himself wryly, the type of stunt you would pull if you were trying to get over to the post office to buy stamps.

After another long suck on his cigarette B looked down the road past the bank and the fruit shop. A stooped-over woman in a duck egg blue cardigan and a ruffled blouse was shuffling past the paper shop. She was laden down on each side by plastic bags of tins and other shopping. In her slipstream, and even more bent double with her head resolutely fixed on the pavement was a second woman. She was wearing a cardigan in the same style, but a darker blue. B was amused by this. What's the odds on that, the same clothes on two women on the same street?

As the women edged closer to where he was standing one face and then the second became visible. The same pinched noses, watery green eyes and grey hair raised in buns. Sisters. Each seemed oblivious to the presence of the other but they were pulled up the hill towards the roundabout by the same invisible umbilical cord. Destined always to be together.

The heater above the door blew hot, fetid air on B as he went back in to the betting shop. The sickly blast disconcerted him momentarily, just like it always did. He hated that sense of passing from one world to another, the change it represented. Going from where he had been to where he was supposed to go. Part of him always wanted to stay just where he was forever. Nothing bad could happen there. To go somewhere else, to leave your hiding place, was always a risk. Change is not good and never was. He clung to that mantra as his comfort blanket, his shelter from the world. The problem for him now was that it was bringing him less and less comfort and security as time just drifted on.

A resigned calm had now descended over the shop. The initial excitement that always accompanied money in the pocket, a fresh bundle of dockets and the pile of sharpened pencils on the counter had dissipated. Every beaten docket flung petulantly to the floor only let more air out of the balloon. It was a different place at mid-day to what it soon became once the losing bets started to accumulate. B knew the pain of a loser in the first and the way it fucked up your Lucky 15. All hope gone and gone early.

After the first raft of losing horses and dogs attention shifted to the football coupons – three aways, six draws, ten homes, everyone had their way of doing them. Trying to find a way to figure out the puzzle was now at the front of the collected minds. The football bets were popular because they offered the possibility of delayed gratification and the sense that all their secrets would only be given up when all the results were in.

Forfar 4 East Fife 5. B smiled to himself. When was that one going to come in? After all his years in here he was still waiting for that result to be read. His smile must have been a little too manic because he could feel a couple of the men hanging around at the pay-out window gawping at him. Fuck them.

All around they were digging in for the long haul. The dream of flush of early winners had not materialised. This was not going to be one of those days where you backed one after another until closing time and then the party moved across the road for the winnings to be disposed of. For most those days never came and they consoled themselves with the thought that in the long run it didn't really make any difference. It was always destined to end in the same way. An empty pocket.

The gathering air of resignation was broken by the whoop of a young fella whose eyes had been fixed hard on a dog race from Sunderland. You fucking little dancer. He skipped his way towards the pay-out window and in a wholly unselfconscious way clicked his heels and pushed his arms up in the air.

Who does your man think he is? Fred fucking Astaire. B had seen that move some place before. It was way back though. Way, way back. They had been on holiday, somewhere out to the west.

He should have been able to remember when it was because they didn't go away every year. Only if there was work, his da used to say. We can only afford to go if I have work to come back to. And that wasn't every year.

He was 13 or 14 and he'd gone off on his own for a walk down towards the beach after they'd had their dinner. Where had they been staying? It wasn't in a house so it must have been that pokey wee caravan they borrowed from someone from time to time. He couldn't remember who owned it. He hated the way they were all cooped up together so much that he had got hold of an old army-issue tent to sleep in from somewhere. After pestering them all for so long he was eventually allowed to pitch it outside. His own space at last. Hard ground to lie on but at least it was his hard ground. The caravan was parked up on the hill overlooking the stony beach and the tent was just in behind.

To their left was the stone pier and beyond that a mile of yolk-yellow sand. That was where he was headed. He loved the way it stretched out in front of him, all full of possibilities. There didn't seem room for anything bad. The way ahead looked golden.

It was quiet. The day's ceaseless mizzling rain had seen to that. But just over the islands the clouds were starting to part and there was the occasional glimpse of the dying sun in between the pillows of grey. B clambered over the rocks, pleased at his own dexterity. Our own wee goat, his ma had said. Some goat. Da always had to have the last word but he didn't think he meant anything by it. Not that time anyway.

As he got closer to the sand he could see a tall, skinny boy, maybe a few years older than him. Using his bare feet and toes he was marking out a square. His big toe seemed to be the line marker. Halfway along he jarred his foot on a buried stone or shell, grimaced for a second and then continued on, now using his heel to fill out the line. If he was aware of B watching him, he didn't let it show. In his bubble of concentration nobody else mattered.

B thought he knew what was going on. They had set up a make-shift tennis court on this same patch of hard sand many times before. One of them would be Năstase, the other Borg. There was a pair of battered old rackets in a cupboard in the caravan and they'd been able to buy yellow-haired balls in the shop at the top of the hill that sold Kilimanjaro lollies.

So this guy was the advance party and the others would be down in a bit, maybe from one of the other caravans pitched in the valley between the roads, the pier and the dunes. His job was to mark out the court and his reward would be first game. Winner stays on as well.

But when he looked a bit closer, there were no other lines apart from the outside square. No service line. No net. This wasn't tennis, that much was clear. The tall, skinny boy was standing at one corner of the square, just outside where the lines met. He stretched up to his full height to pull off a loose-fitting, long-sleeved top. Then, reaching down, he pulled off his grey sweat bottoms. A self-contained bubble of perpetual motion he was stretching constantly, this way and that. B could see that he was now wearing a pair of white shorts and vest of the same colour. He was transfixed. The silence of the scene was all enveloping, broken only by the lap-lap chatter of outgoing tide.

Then, in a mighty whoosh of activity, the tall, skinny boy took three sprinting strides from the corner of the square towards its middle and launched himself into the air, flipping over once before landing on his feet inches from the opposite corner. He took a quick breath and then repeated the manoeuvre, only in the opposite direction. Gymnastics? Here? Here?

The combination of the tall, skinny boy's total absorption and the sheer physicality of what he was doing made B feel like a voyeur, an intruder. By hunching his shoulders slightly over it was as if he was trying to make himself less obviously visible but it didn't really matter. Other than B, he had no audience.

His routine now in full swing, this tall, skinny boy was oblivious to everything except his own physical domination of this deserted, beautiful beach. Warmed up now, he was cartwheeling – or at least

B thought that was what it was – from one end of the square to the other and back again. As time had gone on, he had introduced an element of precision to his movements, most particularly to the way he landed when the move or routine was completed.

Grace and control on landing. B remembered the phrase from a lost morning in front of the television during the last school holidays watching the Olympics. There was a Russian girl – or was she Romanian – who he had developed a terrible crush on and he just loved to watch her rise and fall like froth blown off a wave. But that was the Olympics. This was now.

And so it went on. Almost afraid to blink in case it would break the spell, B stood watching and feasting on what was playing out in front of him. Now fully engrossed in the rhythm and the ebb and flow of the performer's movement, he could sense it was reaching its end. Disappointment like he had never felt before began to well up in him. Inside, he was willing and urging himself to remember every detail, every jump, twist and turn. This was visual food for hungry times later.

The tall, skinny boy was now creating his own sense of drama. Standing still at the corner furthest away from where B was, he took a deep, exaggerated pull of air and closed his eyes. Then, with a final explosion of activity he ran, flipped forward and landed in what seemed like one beautiful fluid blur. His finished movement on to the hardened sand just at the tide-line was foot perfect. He opened his eyes, smiled out to the sea and then walked contentedly back to where he'd left his top and bottoms. The show was over. B felt so uncontrollably bereft that he thought he was going to cry there and then.

TWELVE

Are you getting in or what?

B didn't move. He stayed leaning against the lamp-post, kicking metronomically at his left boot with his right. A small patch of leather on the steel toe-cap had worn away and he was trying to make the fissure bigger with his other foot. Kick, kick, kick.

I said, are you getting in or what. There's other people waiting here.

B looked up, caught the driver's eye briefly and moved forward.

Hope you've the right money. You've wasted enough of my time already.

The coins dropped from B's limp hand to the driver's, like they were shaking half-heartedly at the start of a football match. There was a free double seat near the back. The bus smelt of disrupted sleep, agitation and hairspray. B pulled the sleeve of his coat down so he could wipe away the mist on the window to look outside. He needn't have bothered.

As if piqued by the unnecessary delay to his timetable at the last stop, the driver of the bus was now going faster than he needed to, then breaking at the last minute before every approaching stop. Everyone lurched forward, as if on cue, breaking their collective movement by reaching out to the seat in front.

B fiddled self-consciously with his tie and reached up to undo the top button. The stale, exhaled air was making him feel sick. Why had he bothered with the tie anyway? He was only forced to dress like this on special occasions, wakes and funerals mostly. No weddings yet. The imperfect viewing circle he had made on the window was starting to cloud up again. Drops of condensation were now moving down through the middle of it. B absentmindedly traced the shape of a heart in the newly-formed film of water. With a flourish, he drew an arrow from one corner to the other. Then he stopped. He should have bought a paper before getting on. That would have passed the time a bit. He shut his eyes. When he opened them the empty seat next to him had been filled by a woman his mother's age. Her tartan shopping trolley was balanced precariously on her knees.

> They should have an extra one on at busy times, she said, to no-one in particular.

She had the look of someone who spoke a lot to no-one in particular. B didn't answer and turned his head away from her perfume and towards the window. The combination of the stop-start of the bus and the assault of different smells was making him feel even sicker now. He should have eaten something. The lunch his mother had left out for him the night before had been dumped in the bin beside the bus-stop and he was regretting that now. Still. No work today, so no lunch. That was a stupid way to think, though, wasn't it? He hadn't been thinking. Or maybe thinking too much.

The bus coughed to a final stop and the slow procession towards the door at the front began. B sat his ground and let the others get off first. He always liked to do that but he wasn't really sure why. When he eventually got up beside the driver's seat he could hear him muttering to himself as he counted the coins out of his dispenser.

> He'll be on my fucking back again, that inspector. Wasn't even my fault we were late.

There were three or four people in front of him in the queue for security at the front door. He could just see the policeman through the bodies checking the pockets and bags. His face was a mixture of surliness and restlessness. He never made eye contact with the people he was checking. Instead, his eyes seemed to dart all around as if looking for threats real or imagined. It was as if death or misfortune was just around the corner and he was readying himself for it. By now B had reached the main door. No matter how many times he went through this process, he couldn't help himself. Resentment just bubbled to the surface.

Arms, barked the policeman.

B's were already up, in crucifix pose.

Legs.

Two leather-gloved hands padded roughly along the inside of his body, along the back of his trousers and then down his legs.

Feet.

B didn't move, deliberately forcing a reaction.

Feet, I said. This time he lifted first one boot, then the other to show his soles. No need to play the smart boy, son. Go on.

The air inside was a stale and as sickly as on the bus earlier, only this time with added hostility and desperation. All around there were pockets of people – mostly men – huddling conspiratorially and looking nervously out. The same meerkat eyes as the policeman at the door, only separated by circumstance. These men were the picture of inaction. The few movements and gestures there were appeared exaggeratedly slow, as if to emphasise their levels of disengagement with this place and this process. By contrast, every now and then well-dressed men in suits and ties would inject some movement into the static tableau. The busiest – and you could pick those out straight away – moved from group to group, exchanging false pleasantries and imparting information.

Tommy. Back again, I see. We'll be on down there in about ten minutes. Listen out for your name.

Sean. What is it this time? Same carry on as before?
Anyway, we'll fix it up between us, won't we?

They got very little back in response, just the occasional Aye
or You know. The gap in social class and total absence of any
common ground beyond this space they were occupying was clear.
They had been thrown together only by events. This was a symbiotic
relationship, like the sparrow picking ticks out the back of the hippo.
These relationships were never going to be more than business,
despite the faux-friendliness of the sparrows and their suits.

The only women B could see were gathered around an upright,
dirty-brown coffee machine. Smoke rose up from the group to form
a mocking halo. They lacked the belligerent insouciance of the
men and gave off a definite air of something being missing, not
quite right. Despite the crowds all around them, it was the absence
of men that seemed to define them. The absence of their men.
Every now and then, two or three peeled away in response to a
muddled announcement over the tannoy. They disappeared through
heavy slatted wooden doors, then emerged a minute, maybe two,
later blinking to readjust to the daylight which leaked in from the
dirty windows that ran the length of the hall. Their day was over and
they had their next date. Their own sentence. Some of the younger
women struggled to keep control of babies and crying toddlers.
It was only the children who seemed able to muster any enthusiasm
for this place, this new playground. The innocence of their playing
and running served as vivid counterpoint to the fetid fog of cynicism
which hung over everything and everyone. This was not a place for
them, not a place for the carefree.

B squinted at the typed sheets of white paper pinned haphazardly to
the walls outside each of the rooms. Like war-time lists of the dead
and missing. He scanned the names printed beside each number
running from one to a hundred and beyond. He had no idea why he was
doing this. Maybe it was just to give the illusion that he belonged, that
he was in the right place and that he fitted in with all of these people.
In reality, he had never felt more out of place and alone in his life.

In the absence of anything better to do, and to make it look like he at least knew what he was supposed to be doing, he pushed against a door with a brass plaque that read Number Two. The door didn't give completely at first and when he pushed a little harder he found his way blocked by the outstretched arm of another policeman. They were everywhere. B could just about see inside. Facing him, but with their backs to everyone else in the room, were two dishevelled looking men. They were both about his age, maybe a little younger, but they looked tired and resigned. A stern-faced man wearing a black gown was talking to them, reading out a succession of names and dates and referring to this law of this date and that law of another. He was clearly irritated by the way they were refusing to look at him but was doing his very best not to show it. At the end of his litany of alleged wrongs, he paused for what was clearly dramatic purpose. It didn't have the effect he desired.

What do you have to say to these allegations?

The level of chatter and formless noise diminished for a few seconds as if the stage was being cleared for the big response. It didn't come. Almost in unison, but not quite, the two men began speaking in Irish. B couldn't understand what they were saying but it didn't really matter. Before they had even finished, the attention of the room had moved away. B strained to hear above the renewed hubbub.

….if they decline to…we have a duty to enter on their behalf…take them down.

The men disappeared down steps, shouting now with their fists clenched and raised to – it seemed – no-one in particular.

What number are you here for? the policeman asked.

B didn't answer and turned away, anxious to make it obvious that he had only come in by mistake and had nothing to do with any of what had just gone on. Most of all he wanted to show that he didn't really belong here.

There were fewer people right at the end of the long hall. B walked up three steps into another waiting area. This time there was only one ornate door, in the same dark wood as before. It was quieter here as well, more reserved and less frantic. The people who were there didn't seem to stand around in the same pre-determined groups. They were clearly identifiable as families who were hunched in together for comfort and support. There was none of the furtive, stabbing looking around that characterised the public area he had just come from. The staff who were standing around seemed a little more polite too, more respectful and less on edge. The collective mood seemed more reflective and relaxed, as if the worst had already happened to everyone there. This was the Coroner's Court B had been looking for.

Every now and then a kind-faced, middle-aged woman came out of the double doors and quietly announced a family name. O'Hagan. Wilkinson. O'Kane. Then, in direct response to the call, one of the family groupings would move noiselessly towards her in unison, their heads bowed as if in prayer. They disappeared inside and the doors closed noiselessly except for the faintest swish of pushed-out air. Their time in there seemed to take about ten minutes. They then re-emerged. Some of them were crying. Nobody seemed to walk without either their arm around someone else or with arms around them. They were holding on to each other as a way of not falling apart. This was what collective grief looked like. B knew he was in the right place.

He went inside. The room was laid out as before but the atmosphere was less frenetic. It was as if everything here had already been decided and was already known. This was about how it had happened. A man about his boss's age sat in a chair above everyone else. He was wearing a gown like the man before, but it had a white fur collar. He looked tired but alert. It was the face of a man who had heard everything that was about to unfold hundreds of times before but who knew he couldn't let that show. Each time had to be like the first to every new family who presented themselves in front of him. He bore a look of forced but genuine respect. B found a seat right at the end of one of the long wooden benches. The curve of the wood pushed against the top of his thighs. The woman beside him was crying.

Proper, uncontrolled tears, the sort he had only ever seen before at funerals or wakes. He leant forward just a little to hear what was being said but could only pick out snatches.

> …the cause of death was a single bullet wound, entry point lower left chest…it travelled upwards through the left lung and other organs before exiting at the shoulder…the exit wound was the size of a ten pence piece…death would have followed very soon afterwards. Has the bullet been analysed?
>
> Yes. We believe the gun used to fire it was used in two other killings in the past 18 months.
>
> And the criminal investigation?
>
> It remains open but unsolved. We have no active lines of enquiry.

As the questions were posed and answered, two rows of men in suits of different ages wrote down what was being said without ever once looking up. As time passed, the voices and the details became little more than background noise for B. He couldn't really pay attention for any period of time and the entire experience reminded him of nothing more than being back at school. The first part of any lesson he made it to – Maths, English, it didn't really matter – would be fine and he had little or no problem following what was going on. But bit by bit he would drift away into a world where the equations or the figures of speech became only a vague humming in his ear. It was not an unpleasant sensation but it rendered everything that followed wholly useless and without purpose.

By now he was looking at the legal people lined up beside each other, while the words just washed over him. What were they called? Solicitors, that was it. He could see there was an obvious pecking order. The most important sat nearest to the front and listened – or pretended to listen – to what was being said above them. To do this they put one hand, sometimes two, under their chins to give the impression that they were really paying attention. Behind them a row of younger, eager men, some the same age as himself, were

83

writing non-stop, clearly wanting to show that they too valued the importance of every word. He could only see one girl in amongst this sea of blue and black suits. She wrote intently and at the same speed as the others.

The boy sitting next to her kept leaning in towards her to whisper something and then laugh exaggeratedly at his own joke. She seemed wholly detached from him and never once laughed back. The boy looked like someone from round his way that he knew, who was it? He couldn't place him. What was his name? What was it? The Sprinter. The Sprinter, that's what he was known as. The story was that he had been caught robbing an old woman's flat by her son but that he had got away because he was far too quick for him. It turned out he had been far and away the best runner in his class, cross-country mostly, and won everything at the school sports day. His problem was that even though he got away easily, he had been recognised. So when the squad came for him, the lead man told him: This would normally be a one knee job, but we heard how quick you were able to run away so we need to slow you down a bit. So they blasted a hole in the other knee as well. When the story got re-told during the tea break the next day someone said that would put the running out of him. B didn't laugh. And he thought the laughter around him was too laced with fear to be real.

So, the Sprinter, that's who he looked like, this drip in the suit. The business of the day was going on all around them but B had lost his way, his compass, completely. It was all just a thick soup of words to him now. Background noise. Death was instantaneous. 9mm pistol. Skull particles on the footpath. Left a wife and three children. Responsibility wasn't claimed.

There was a short break. Small pockets of conversation broke out around the room. Then the disinterested but self-important clerk coughed in the exaggerated way teachers used to try when they were trying to get a class back under control.

The Coroner calls the case of Peter Friel.

B stiffened. He was back lying there, coffin still, waiting to be found, waiting to be killed. This was what he had come for. Why had he come?

Mr Coroner. The clerk looked up and then behind.

Thank you. Who is here to prove the circumstances and time of death?

He spoke in a detached, respectful way. B got the impression that he had asked this question many times before. Part of his job was to make it sound like the first time. A policeman excused his way along a row of people just to B's right. He held his stiff-brimmed cap in his right hand like a theatrical prop. Or a crutch.

The clerk spoke again.

You are already sworn this morning, constable.

And he began.

Peter Friel was a 19-year-old man from the west of the city. He was a trainee shipping clerk. On the night in question he had agreed to run an errand for his grandmother. A delivery driver had been unable to get to her home because of rioting which had blocked the road and she was waiting for a new hall and stair carpet. Peter offered to go and collect it from the shop. He arrived at the carpet shop at approximately 5.30pm and was served by a Mr Scott, the owner. We have spoken to him. The two men exchanged a joke about whether the deceased was really going to be able to balance the roll of carpet on his shoulder.

A sound, like an involuntary, forced-back shudder broke the monotone flow. B looked and could see it had come from a woman, maybe his mother's age, who was now enveloped in the arms of a much younger girl. Maybe it was the word deceased that had set her off, he thought.

The policeman started again.

A number of people have come forward to say they saw the…He checked himself… Saw Mr Friel walking with the carpet and remarked on the unusual nature of the scene.

B remembered it like something out of those Saturday morning silent comedies.

One witness – who has made it clear they do not want to be named – was stopped by Mr Friel to ask for directions. It would appear that he had taken a wrong turn on the way to his grandmother's house.

The policeman paused and fumbled with the pages and notes in front of him.

Yes continue, the Coroner said kindly, without looking up from the thick, leather-clad book in which he was writing.

Thank you, sir. The next and final piece of information we have is from a woman who lives on the street where the body was found. She was standing on a chair at a front bedroom window fixing curtains, which had been pulled down by her children earlier while playing, back on to a curtain rail. The young man, balancing this long piece of carpet on his shoulder, caught her eye at the top of the street. At the other end of the street three men, with scarves around their necks but not covering their faces, came out of a side alley and stood facing him. They shouted but she couldn't hear what was said. The man with the carpet stood still. She could see one other person on the street. He was described as a workman, carrying a lunch bag. The woman in the house was too far away to see anyone's face. The man was walking in the same direction as Mr Friel, but was a distance ahead of him. When he saw the other three men at the top of the street he jumped over a fence behind which there was waste ground. She did not see this man again.

The policeman paused and looked into the body of the courtroom.

We have tried unsuccessfully to find this second witness. We believe he has important and compelling testimony

> to give as he could potentially identify the other
> three men.

B could feel acidic bile rising from his stomach to the back of his throat. For so long this had been something he imagined had happened to someone else, that he was just an observer looking in at what was going on. This was too real. Too real.

> The woman in the house – our Witness A – saw the men pulling the scarves up and over their faces. Two of them pulled long kitchen-type knives out of their jackets. All three of them then ran towards Mr Friel. Witness A pulled the curtains closed and went downstairs. She was, and is, terrified.

> Thank you, constable. Can you now move on to the circumstances and cause of death.

> The next information we have is that Mr Friel's body was lying in the street for approximately a further hour after the last evidence provided by Witness A. There are intelligence reports that masked men were in the immediate area throughout this period. When police arrived they found his body wrapped roughly in the carpet he had been carrying. Mr Friel had been stabbed thirteen times.

Reaching under the chair on which he was sitting the policeman lifted an envelope and handed it up to the clerk who, in turn, passed it to the Coroner.

> These are the photographs of the injuries taken at the post mortem. The face and body were so disfigured that the coffin could not be opened prior to burial. This obviously added to the anguish and distress of his family.

Another shudder from the benches beside him. B didn't dare look around.

> And what is your working theory in relation to ̄s
> terrible crime?

This was a motiveless, senseless and barbaric sectarian attack, in our view. Nothing more and nothing less. We have no leads or further information at this time. The evidence of Witness A is not enough to secure convictions due to her distance away from the three men she saw. However, the testimony of the second, as yet unidentified witness, and his potential ability to identify the perpetrators is clearly of central importance to the case we would wish to present to a court. We have not found this man and he has not come forward. We would appeal for him to do so and offer him as much protection as is possible if he does.

B opened his hands on his lap and stared vacantly at them. He swallowed some of the sick that was still welling up at the back of his throat and looked up again. The older woman he had seen crying before was now sitting where the policeman had been. She was asked her name and spoke quietly in response. Her words seemed to disappear into the air around her.

I only have one son. I miss him terribly. But we get comfort because he was doing a good thing when this bad thing was done to him. That kind of keeps us going. My mother, his grandmother, blames herself though. She has gone downhill badly and we're worried that she'll never really recover.

The clerk handed her a piece of paper and she was asked to sign it. She went to write but the pen barely touched the page or made a mark, as if she could not complete this final act of her son's life.

Thank you, Mrs Friel. The court offers its condolences.

The Coroner was speaking again. He was doing his best to sound sincere but there was a weariness in his voice, as if the repetitiveness of the horror and the disgust was slowly but surely wearing him out.

Your son was the victim of a horrible, sectarian murder. He was an innocent man in the wrong place with the most evil of people at the wrong time. I do not know how they sleep at night. This murder remains unsolved, but there is clearly a witness, Witness B, who can help you to find closure to your suffering. Only he knows why he will not make himself known to the police. I would implore him to do so.

THIRTEEN

Dad, you said the last one would be the end. Come on. Please.

To B's left looking up at the newspaper pages of runners and form pinned to the wall was a man he recognised from around the shop. B didn't know his name. Or if he had at one time, he didn't any more. Another one in a long list.

He was the sort of man you would remember having seen before, though. Built like a wee boy who had grown up too quickly, that was the best way of describing him. Maybe five feet tall, at a push, but slight and childlike in his features and his body. His hair was cut in a close crop which seemed only to emphasise how much like a schoolboy he actually looked. Blow hard at him and he might fall over. He was tanned, swarthy even. The word was he spent a lot of time in Spain during the summer and kept a lot of his colour from then.

How he could afford to take those trips was anyone's guess because he was an absolutely terrible punter. It wasn't just that he lost. When he lost, he lost big. Four or five hundred in an afternoon would be no big deal for him. But it was worse than that. The consensus about him was that he was just unlucky, plain and simple. Unlucky in his own punting, unlucky to be betting beside. You just got people like that sometimes. Superstition was part of the culture of this place and the cloud of misfortune that followed him around was not one anybody wanted to be caught under.

The young boy was always with him. B always paid special attention to him and he didn't really know why. His vulnerability was there for all to see, the product of years of trying and failing to look after his father. The obvious reversal of the natural order was what made people feel sorry for both of them. But B didn't. There was no need. The role the young boy had been forced to take forged something strong within him that he would carry easily for the rest of his life. B saw that and he didn't think anyone else did.

After all the anxiety, this worry about what the man who was supposed to be taking care of him was going to do next, nothing in the future could ever be as bad again.

> Just let me have a go at this last one. I've been following him all year and the trainer is on a good run. I've got a good feeling about today.

As his father scribbled on the betting slip, the young boy patted him gently on the bottom of his back. The contact was so slight, the man didn't even notice. But B did. After all this is over, nothing will be as bad again.

> What's in the bag?
> Stuff.
> What kind of stuff?
> Just stuff.

And so conversation at the betting rail in front of the screens ground to a halt.

B ignored them and concentrated instead on the next race at Lingfield Park. It was pure shite, he knew that much. A rubbish race, all poor horses with very little or mixed form. A real bookies' holi~ v fund of a race. Still, the betting slip never refuses ink, B thou~

himself as he tried to figure out the puzzle.

Jesus, it's yourself isn't it?

He felt a nudge to his right shoulder. Not forceful, but enough for him to notice. It pushed his hand into making an involuntary mark on the betting slip. He looked down and thought, it's ruined. What a strange way to think.

All that took time and when B looked to his side the man who had just spoken to him was really in his face and in his space. He looked about the same age but better kept, even B could see that. The type of guy who you just knew his wife had a hand in dressing. Just to keep him smart, otherwise he couldn't have cared less.

We were at school together, weren't we? Back in the day. Your name's not coming to me just at the minute, but sure isn't that the sort of thing that happens to boys like us when they get to our age? The memory goes. That, and having to get up for the toilet in the middle of the night. Isn't that right? Do you not remember me at all?

I don't know who the fuck you are or what the fuck you're talking about.

Ah now, don't be like that now. We were pals. Do you not remember? Two rows from the back we used to sit. I was the messer, you were the quiet one. Never much to say for yourself. And we used to play football together, for the club and for the school. I was the rough as a badger full back and you were a nippy, skilful corner forward. The first man I ever saw try a solo dummy. And you took the frees as well, didn't you? You were a good operator. Do you not remember? And what about the Rice Cup. You couldn't play because you'd got your leg cut in some accident with a saw your father had been using at home and then we got absolutely stuffed. I've said to so many people over the years that if we'd had you we could have done some serious damage.

Do you not remember?

B kept looking at the list of horses and didn't meet his gaze, not even for a second. He liked one called Orchard Supreme. Hannon and Hughes together was always a decent combination. He swung around to get a price from the screen. 9/2. Would be a nice wee lift after the day he'd had. And still this man beside him kept talking.

It must be years since I saw you. I was in the States for a while and then in England. Just chasing work basically. But we're back here twenty years now. What about you? Do you live over this side of town now? I'm still over by. Home bird, me. You'll not get me straying too far from there now at my time of life.

The inane chatter was broken by some cheering from in front of the screen showing the dog racing from Sunderland. Someone obviously had a bit of a sweat on one of them and he was making sure he let everybody else know about it. B and the man both turned sideways to look, almost involuntarily drawn by the noise, registered what was happening and then turned back.

And still he kept talking, a little more quietly and conspiratorially this time. As if he was trying to keep a secret.

But then I suppose you had that bit of bother, didn't you? Weren't you away for a while after that fella was killed? That's what I heard anyway, but maybe there was no truth in that. Terrible business. But then I suppose that was what it was like then. A lot of things happened that people would prefer to forget, if only they were let.

He stopped, as if struck by a sudden realisation that this time he had overstepped the mark. B took a step forward and towards him so that his right foot was on top of the man's left one. He leant into him so that their faces were only inches apart.

Listen. I'm trying to have a quiet bet here. I don't know who you are or what the fuck you're talking about. You're right about one thing though. A lot of thir \s went on that people would be better off forge

And this might be a good time and place for you to start. You get me?

He lifted his foot and the man backed away, his face like a scolded dog.

Alright wee man. No need to be like that. I was only trying to be friendly.

FOURTEEN

B pushed at the half-opened door.

        Hello? Are you serving?

From inside he could hear unselfconscious, out-of-tune singing.

        Down by the Salley Gardens.....my true love...

B walked along the corridor until he came to a door on his right. He stopped and looked in. Behind the bar was a round-bellied man, maybe fifty, wearing a pair of black trousers and an off-white t-shirt which was clearly moonlighting as a vest. He had his back to B and was facing towards an ornate mirror hung over the till which was advertising a whiskey B had never heard of.

The barman – for that is what he must be, thought B – had a shaving brush in his right hand. The cream bristles stood proudly out from the thickened, wooden handle. Still singing to himself, the barman reached to one side and swished the shaving brush from side to side in a large brown mug.

The brush emerged covered in shaving soap which the barman then dabbed on to his stubbly growth. He repeated this process three or four times until his face was covered in lather. With his left hand he lifted a stainless steel open razor and started to shave with deft, practised strokes.

> I'll only be a minute, cub, he said, at last registering his customer's presence. Sit down and I'll be with you when I've got this over with.

B looked around. The bar was dark. There were only two sources of natural light that he could see. One was a long, narrow window over the bar area which looked like it could only be opened with some sort of elongated hook. The other was a heavily-patterned embossed window on the wall opposite. A single, naked light bulb hung from the ceiling over the mirror, where the barman was still busying himself. B felt uncomfortable, like he had just happened upon an intensely personal and private act. The barman, though, didn't seem to mind at all.

All the available wall space appeared to be covered with black and white photographs of old football and hurling teams and framed match programmes. A leather football took pride of place on a mahogany ledge that had been fixed incongruously close to a religious picture of the Sacred Heart. The once white ball was now corpse-grey and redolent of long-forgotten adventures.

Four stools covered in blood-red heavy plastic guarded the bar like assiduous footmen. The floor, made up of stone slabs, was rough and uneven except for an irregular polished line which marked the standing positions along the length of the bar counter. This was the public bar. Nothing about it suggested a woman had ever spent any length of time here.

An opening, but with no apparent door, led through to what looked like the lounge. On the far opposite wall, a fire, either newly lit or just being coaxed back to life from the night before, burnt a smoking, orangey red.

> Do you like my GAA stuff, then, cub? Football's the game, though, isn't it?

It was a question asked in a way that didn't really require an answer.

> I don't really bother much with that stick game. I only

have the stuff up there to keep some of the boys who come in happy. They're a fierce narky lot. Sensitive too. But football – you can't beat it.

The main business of the shaving was finished and all that remained were the tidemarks of foam high up on his cheek, behind his ears and down by his Adam's apple. He reached round to the counter for a tea-towel what was sitting beside a basket of empty glasses and wiped anything that remained off his face. The tea-towel was thrown back down on top of the glasses.

With the brown mug in his hand he walked over to the sink and rinsed it out under the tap. Letting the tap run, he filled a kettle sitting on the draining board, plugged it in and flicked the on switch. There was a box of teabags further down the bar. He lifted one, threw it into the same brown mug and stood back waiting for the kettle to boil.

> I can name every All Ireland final team – winners and losers – right back to 1929, the year I was born. The best team I saw was the Cavan team of 1947. You know, the Polo Grounds team. Gannon was the goalie. Full backs, Doonan, O'Reilly and Smith. Then, Wilson, O'Reilly and Deignan. Midfield, Duke and Brady. The half forwards were Tighe Mick Higgins and McDwyer. Full forwards, Stafford, Donohue and O'Reilly. You've heard of Mick Higgins, haven't you, cub? Best centre three quarters I've ever seen anyway. What can I get you? You're early on the go this morning.

B did his best to process all the words and information that were washing over him. All the talking, all the photographs threatened to overwhelm him completely.

> A half-and-half, he said, gesturing first to the stout tap and then to the optics along the wall.
> Surely. Have you been over beyond?
> Aye.
> I do get a few in around this time from over there.

97

It's a hard place to be these days with all this carry-on.
Nothing too serious, I hope, anyway?

B didn't answer. Just give me the drinks and spare me the interrogation. Undeterred, the barman continued his one man show.

Do you see that shirt there? He was pointing down towards the wall that separated the bar from the lounge. That's from a county final played over thirty years ago now. If you look closely enough you can just see the blood on the shoulder. That came from the mouth of the boy I gave a clatter to. He didn't see it coming. And there wasn't another word out of him afterwards.

He set the half-pint glass and the spirits tumbler down on the bar, turned to his left to fill a small jug with water and set it beside the drinks. B sucked on the whiskey and smarted at the alcoholic shock as it hit the back of his throat. The warmth that quickly followed, though, was the pay-off. He sipped at the stout to take away the taste but the combination of them both in his stomach made him feel momentarily nauseous.

A repeat of the same drinking sequence made him feel a bit better and he began to ease into his stool. The first waves of the alcohol had dulled him just a little and enough for him to realise that he was now on show in front of this barman. To maintain the dynamic between them he would now have to contribute to the conversation. Just to pass himself, as he'd heard his mother say so many times before during one of his long silences at family dinners.

I'm sure you hear all sorts of stuff and nonsense in here?

There. That wasn't so bad, was it? And it had the desired effect.

Aye, well, you know. Sometimes people just blabber on and forget I'm here, listening. The worst rows are about football. Everyone's usually too afraid to talk about politics and all of that other stuff. Just in case they say the wrong thing. You know how it is. Do people ever tell you about things they've seen – you know, bad stuff – that they haven't told anybody else about?

B had steered the exchange in this direction and he wasn't really sure why. Both of his drinks were almost finished now and the dread he had been experiencing all morning in court was starting to ease and fog over. He was starting to lose sight of the terror he always carried with him and he was enjoying the sensation of being unburdened, however temporarily.

Sometimes, cub, but the mouths are the ones to be wary of. Can't hold their water. If they're talking it's usually a sign that they don't know as much as they think they do. It's the quiet ones I look out for. I have a boy comes in here most nights. Same routine every time – six pints and a rum to finish off. He never says a word outside of ordering his drinks and just sits there in the corner, head down. One night there, around Christmas I think it was, when I was closing up, I found him sitting on one of the toilets in there. The door to the cubicle was open. Crying he was, just sitting there crying to himself. I gathered him up, settled him down and got him out the door home. The next night he was in there wasn't a word about it, not even a look or any sign of anything being wrong at all. Not a flicker. So I just served him and away he went again, same as before.

B closed his eyes. How good would that be, just to tell someone, to lift the horse collar of what he had seen from around his neck and just tell someone. The urge to do that threatened to overwhelm him. They had done this thing at school way back. It usually happened after lunch. The teacher would tell them to put their elbows on the desk, lay their heads down on top of them and close their eyes.

Imagine you're somewhere very pleasant. That'll be different for each one of you. But it should be a place where there is no noise and where there are no distractions. If you can get into that state it will help you get closer to God.

This was usually met by some muffled sniggers from each of the five rows of boys in the classroom, until eventually the ripples joined together into a flood of derisory laughter.

Right, that's enough, you ungrateful little bastards. I don't know why I bother.

By this time all pretence of meditation had been abandoned and the class had descended into raucous uproar. But B was always one of the last to raise his head. He would have liked to have stayed outside of the real world for just a bit longer. He loved the prospect of freedom, the allure of weightlessness.

The moment was gone and he was back in this lonely, dark room staring down at the floor. How long had his eyes been closed for? He didn't know. As he got his bearings again he noticed two fresh glasses in front of him. The pair he had been drinking from were bobbing, then sinking, into the soapy water of the sink underneath the bar. He watched them disappear.

I didn't, ah, I didn't.... B fumbled in his trouser pocket for change.

Don't worry, cub, I stood those for you. Looks like they're going to a good place.

B coughed to cover up the choked-up feeling at the back of his throat. He wasn't going to cry, was he? Not here. Not fucking crying,

Thank you. Thanks.

They exchanged embarrassed looks and then moved their eyes away just as quickly. This was tender as it was going to get. This was as tender as it had been in a long, long time.

A man blustered through the door into the bar, a flailing activity of arms and legs.

Set me up a pint quickly, squire, will you? Badly needed here.

Jesus, citizen, that's one fine entrance.

I have a drouth on me like the bottom of a birdcage.

Quit the talking and get pouring.

The new arrival took an ignorant slurp out of the pint which had been hurriedly set in front of him. There was no ceremony or fanfare. This was utilitarian drinking. The repeat of a ritual.

> That's better, he said, rubbing the back of his left hand over his mouth to get rid of the errant cream. Who's this one with a face on him like a wet week?

He was pointing towards B.

> I've not seen you in here before.

The barman shook his head and gestured with his eyes towards B's stool. Taking the hint, the new man adopted a different line.

> I suppose he's been boring you with football talk from the second you set foot in here?

B lifted his head from his drinks and made eye contact for the first time.

> I don't know too much about it, to be honest.

> Well, you're in good company here then, the barman said, visibly pleased to be able to lift the mood and change the tone.

> Get away out of that.

He swallowed another huge gulp of his pint. Taking two steps back he put the glass down on the counter and slammed his now empty hands, knuckles down, on to the bar.

> Shovels. Hands like shovels. That's what they called them when I was playing and at myself. I could leap like a salmon and field ball all day long. Not a bother. Men who were marking me used to send for a pencil and paper so they could take notes about how good I was. Unmarkable, that's what they used to say about me. Unplayable, more like.

The barman was enjoying this now. The tedium of the morning was lifting. This was familiar ground, back and forward across the bar. None of the uncomfortableness from before.

> They did have a name for you, alright, cub. The clabbercart. You were that slow boys would be able to go and do a message and still be back in time to get the ball off you.

> You're like a lot of the boys that come in here. The longer
> you've not been playing the better you seem to get.

B was smiling now as he tried to wrap himself up in the warm blanket of the verbal parrying. Anything that helped get him out of his own head. The way they were going on reminded him of the boys at work. He needed to get back to all that soon. To where he could be safe.

The bar filled with noon-time drinkers. For each there was a greeting, sometimes barbed but always laced with affection and warmth as the burly arms of the space opened up again to welcome newcomers.

> Two more, cub?

B shook his head. He felt warmed inside, better, but he had had enough for now. Any more and the comfortable numbing would be replaced quickly with the jabs of nagging self-doubt. Clouds of cigarette smoke filled the air and the barman reached under the bar for a long wooden pole. Reaching up, he used the hook on the end of it to push open the window over the till.

B could just get a glimpse of the mussel-grey sky outside. A watery, pale winter moon was sliding away, supplanted by the establishing day. He slid off his seat and slipped out the door. Nobody noticed he had gone. Another ghost leaving the stage.

FIFTEEN

The fifty pence piece stuttered through the slot at the right hand side of the soup machine and careered uncertainly down its insides before clunking into the money basket at the bottom.

B looked at the display window. Please make your selection. Vegetable or beef. Press 1 for vegetable. Press 2 for beef. Vegetable or beef. Beef or vegetable. He was stuck rigid to the spot. An anxious look over his shoulder established that there was no-one waiting. No pressure then. Only from inside. Come on for fuck's sake, make up your mind. Vegetable or beef. It's not exactly the decision of the century.

He stood looking at the machine. Vegetable or beef. Beef or vegetable. His eyes filled with tears. He was a six-year-old boy again. One Saturday morning – it must have been winter because it was dark when they had left the house – his father had walked him into town. They went past the row of shops where the fruit and veg man was just starting to put out his stalls of soup mix and potatoes. Past the butcher's shop where a burly man with a blood-spattered white coat was heaving huge sides of beef off a lorry, on to his shoulder and in through the double doors.

A little further along was where the taxis pulled up. The front seats of each of them were empty and the drivers were propped up against their cars smoking and gossiping. His father nodded to the men he knew and they nodded, almost imperceptibly, in reply. Not a word was exchanged. Beyond them, buses dribbled into the depot in disconsolate ones and twos.

Here we are, he said eventually.

They had stopped outside the only bike shop B had ever seen. He had never been inside but on his way back from school he had often run his fingers over the bikes that were chained together outside. It was a repeated, ritual act of longing for something that was so utterly unobtainable. He looked up at his father. The look said, why are we here? What are we doing here?

Come on, I want to show you something.

The shop smelt of rubber and glue and a Calor Gas heater. It took both of them to readjust to the pungency after the clean, morning air. All around them bikes in various stages of either decay or resurrection rested against one another. Steel wheel frames, denuded of their tyres hung from a pulley attached to one side of the ceiling. Airless and lifeless rubber tubes faced them like expectant suitors on a parallel length of wire attached to the side wall.

A head emerged from a fog of cigarette smoke and tea steam that seemed to be coming from underneath the counter.

Ach, it's yourself. You said you'd be in today, didn't you? Is this the young fella?

Aye.

Come through.

Placing one hand lightly on his right shoulder, his father guided him through the opening to the left of the till. The workshop on the other side was even more chaotic and ramshackle than the relative order of the room they had just walked through. All B could see, stacked up everywhere he looked, was a tangle of bike frames, wheels and chains. The room was lit by a single naked bulb which seemed to hang from the only available space above them. This place smelt differently as well. Decay and rust. This was where the old bikes had been taken to die. It was colder as well.

I have them through here somewhere.

With as much showmanship as he could muster in such unlikely surroundings the man wheeled two bikes forward and clutched the handlebars of each triumphantly on either side of him.

I've worked these back to a decent condition. They were in poor enough shape when I got my hands on them. And you can see that they newly sprayed, one red and one blue. I only finished the blue one last night. My breathing's wrecked with the fumes.

B looked up at his father. He was confused.

Which one do you like? There's no way I can afford one but I thought we might think about starting to save for one for next summer.

B feasted on both of them. But within a few seconds any feeling of contentment had passed and he was consumed with doubt and indecision. Red or blue. Blue or red. He felt a burning in his stomach and had to press his nails hard into the palm of his hand to stop himself crying. Blue or red. Red or blue.

I love both of them. But red, I suppose.

Good job.

The men exchanged knowing looks and B was ushered back out the way he had come in, first out into the relative order of the shop and from there out to the street. He was confused. What was all this about?

Right. We'll go up this way so I can get a paper.

His father continued like nothing had happened.

Not another word about their expedition passed between them. Over time B himself forgot about it until, eventually, he wasn't even sure if it had happened at all.

He reached out his right hand and gripped on to the side of the machine for support. His thumb pressed blindly at one of the buttons.

A paper cup dropped inelegantly from the innards and a stream of foul-coloured liquid flowed from the spout. He had made his decision. But he didn't even know what it was.

The voice on the TV screen was announcing the next race, the 2.30 from Lingfield Park. B looked and listened to the names of the horses, trainers and jockeys, but with detachment. His eye was instead drawn towards the young boy playing the poker machine just to his left. He cupped the soup between his hands and moved towards him. By leaning slightly forward, on to his toes, he could just make himself big enough to peer over the boy's right shoulder to see what was going on.

Each press of the buttons brought an array of multi-coloured playing cards on to the screen. B understood the concept alright – God knows, he had lost enough money playing drunken cards games over the years – but he had never generally bothered with this machine. The boy played it at bewildering speed, placing the same bet of twenty credits each time, processing the cards he was invisibly dealt and then moving on to his next hand.

There didn't seem to be any discernible pattern and the boy seemed to receive neither gratification nor to experience any disappointment at the outcome of each sequence of cards. He played on as if entranced. Out of it, was how B would have described it if he had been asked. But, of course, nobody did. He slurped too hard on the dregs of his soup and burnt the back of his mouth. The noise of the wince he made was enough to make the poker playing boy realise someone was standing watching him. He turned round and glared, all twenty-something menace.

Can I fucking help you out, or what?

It was a question which didn't expect an answer. B shuffled away, an embarrassed voyeur caught looking in the window. He fumbled in his pocket for a betting slip and some change.

50p forecast, 5 and 10 at Lingfield.

Number 5 was the favourite. Orchard Supreme, and he'd coupled it with an outsider, Evens and Odds, one of Kevin Ryan's. He'd always liked Ryan's horses but they always seemed to get better in the sprints. And this race was a mile. Too far probably.

B closed his eyes and wondered if this was what being dead was like. Only it went on for longer. When he opened them again, the race was over and they were putting the result up on the board. His horses had placed fourth and third. Totally fucking useless. The winner was a 14/1 thing, Military Cross. No bastarding good to anyone.

> I could have sat here for a wet week and not picked that one out. One of the men perched on a high stool against the wall spat out the words with a mixture of disgust and resignation.

Nobody was listening. Nobody really cared.

SIXTEEN

It was nearly dark now. B had been walking for a long time but he had no real idea of where he had finished up. He was at the river, he knew that much. To his right there was only gathering darkness. That must be east, he reasoned, because to his left the sun was setting. You're some genius to be able to work that one out. He turned to watch it.

This used to be his favourite thing as a child, when they went on holiday. If they pestered and complained enough they could persuade da to take them down to the pier for one last swim of the day. There was a pre-ordained ceremony to it all. When the discussion was ongoing as to whether they would be able to go or not, da would make a big fuss of rustling through to the back of the paper to check the times of the tides.

> No point going down to dive in if it's going to be too shallow.
>
> Ah, come on, that's not fair.

But they knew. The pages covered all of his face so that only the top of his head poked out at the top. The wait seemed interminable.

You're in luck. High tide was half an hour ago.

Before the words were fully out of his mouth they were piled into the car, a washing-machine jumble of legs and towels. Minutes later they were standing shivering on the pier waiting for the first lemming over the edge which would be the cue for everyone else to tumble in. One jump was enough for B though. The rush of the air in his ears broken by the cold shock of the water. After that he liked to gather an already half-wet towel from the steps of the pier and pull it hurriedly around his shaking shoulders. Then he would turn away from the rest of them to watch the sun sink behind the smallest of the three islands. He'd been told the names of all of them – all the islands – so many times but he could never remember them when it mattered. If it ever mattered at all. So he just called one the big one and the other the small one. The third was the in-between one. He smiled now at the childishness of it all.

Most of all he loved the predictable rise and fall rhythm of it all and the dogged, daily reluctance of the sun to set. And the way, just at the last, that it hung between two towel rails of sky, one above and one below, asserting its rights to the very last second of daylight owed to it.

But now he was stuck and had no idea what to do. The walls were closing in on him. He was losing the will to push back at them. For so long now he had lived the thoughts and memories of what he had seen and what had happened. He had survived and functioned. Now the ground on which he had stood was starting to crumble.

There were options, though, weren't there? Things he could do? What he wanted more than anything was to talk to someone. Just to unburden himself. That would set him free, wouldn't it? Trust in Jesus. His truth will be your release. What a load of balls. He didn't want that sort of release. Not with a priest or anything like that. There were numbers he could phone. He knew that. But what would he say? What could he say? The words were barely formed in his own head. How was he going to be able to arrange them into phrases or sentences that might make sense to someone else? Maybe he could try to get it on paper. I'm going to sit right down and write myself a letter. More nonsense. Who would he send it to? Who would want to read it? Who could possibly want to read his pathetic drivel? The questions kept coming but he was running low on answers. What about getting himself away? On a boat somewhere? Or a plane. He had never been on a plane. This would be as good a time as any. Get away. That was it. Get away to fuck out of here.

Just up from the river there was a road. He didn't know the name of it or where it went. B walked up in that direction. He came up behind what looked like a big, important road sign. It towered above him. He juked under the bottom of it, took a few steps back so he could see and looked up. One arrow – The South. Another – The West. Why hadn't he thought of this before? The road out of here. Lorries and cars, but mostly lorries at this time of night, flew past him like worker ants at intermittent intervals. He had hitched lifts plenty of times before but only when his bus fare had gone on chips or something and he was only going a short way up the road. This was different though. He was going much further.

Pulling his left hand out of his coat pocket he turned square-on to face the oncoming traffic and stuck out his thumb. He wasn't sure of the etiquette, how exactly to do this. Did you keep your hand out continuously or just whenever the cars and lorries were going past? He decided to leave his hand hanging out there on the basis that he was going to look like a total amateur if he was stopping and starting at it. Somebody who didn't really know what he was doing.

He didn't know how long this had been going on but there hadn't even been a flicker of acknowledgement from anyone who drove past. He was the young boy trying to lure the crabs out of the seaweed but they weren't taking the bait. Then it came to him. The reason this wasn't working. You need a fucking sign, man, even just something scribbled on to a bit of cardboard. Just to let them know where you wanted to go. Who was going to stop for him looking like this? Stupid fucking bastard. This was never going to work. He put his two hands up so that they covered almost all his face and crumpled on to his haunches crying uncontrollably.

At first it was one red light drifting across the sky. That plane is flying low, he thought. Or maybe it's a helicopter. Then it was followed by a second. This one was red as well, but more orangey this time. He was transfixed as he traced their paths across the blackness. They stayed the same distance apart but first one and then the other stopped travelling forward and began to drift upwards. It was beautiful. Fire lanterns. Someone had set off two fire lanterns, maybe for a birthday or some other kind of party. A wedding maybe? He hoped it was a birthday, a child's birthday. The best day of anyone's year. Just for you and no-one else.

In the near distance he could see a flashlight. Three men were gathered around it. After a few seconds the middle one slid to the ground against a tree and the other two cocooned in around him. B kept watching them. The man on the ground had cigarette papers balanced delicately on his upturned knees and was crumbling the dregs of a butt on to them. With a degree of ceremony he lit the small lump in his other hand and began to distribute the burnt offerings over the top. Even the slightest noise startled the celebrants as they looked over their shoulders anxiously, like nervous hares.

Come on, come on, someone's going to find us.

The light caught the one who had spoken just under his chin. They weren't men at all. Just boys. Maybe fifteen at most. They had all the lack of poise of young amateurs.

Eventually the ritual was complete and with great reverence they lit up and moved off together. The three amigos, B smiled to himself. He could follow their progress through the gloom by the mobile glow as they passed their chalice between them.

The sense of needing to be somewhere else – anywhere else – and not having the most basic idea of how to get there was now beginning to overwhelm him. If they wanted him they could have him. He just couldn't go on anymore and the pain of that realisation was maybe the worst thing of all. He remembered that crucifying feeling of disappointment from years ago when teams were being picked.

111

I want to be with them, on that team. Why is his name being called out before me? What have I done wrong? What have I done wrong? He always knew the answer to that.

And when it came it was almost a relief, a release. There was now an outlet, a safety valve, for all the upset. There was still something B couldn't work out though. His eyes were open. He knew that because when he blinked he could tell the difference. But he couldn't see anything, only blackness. Slowly he became aware of the physical sensation of something tied around his head and pressing against his eyes. It felt like cloth. And when pieced it all together, he realised what had happened to him. He was blindfolded.

SEVENTEEN

I'm telling you. It's a fucking licence to print fucking money. Take it from me.

B recognised him as someone in the shop who always had something to say but was rarely worth listening to. He was leaning on the shelf at the pay-out window, one eye on the bank of screens in front of him and pontificating to the much smaller, squat man beside him. B didn't know this second man.

I've studied it long and hard. Take it from me.

B knew he definitely wasn't telling the truth now.

In every European game, the bet of a penalty to be given at any time is always over-priced. So if you bet that in every match – one of the two of the teams to be awarded a penalty – you will definitely come out on top over the whole season. I know what I'm talking about.

The world-weary expression on his friend's face suggested the exact opposite but he had been around long enough to know when to nod like one of those toy dogs on a car dashboard.

The penalty kick was invented here you know.

William McCrum was the fella's name. He was the son of the local landowner and he played in goal for the village team. He was so fed up with all the fouling at the last minute to stop goals going in that he came up with the idea of a penalty, a special free kick, if a foul was committed near the goals. It was him who made the suggestion and a few years later it had travelled around the world.

The other two men wheeled around to look at B while he was talking. They had both known him to see around the shop for a long time, years, and had always marked him off as an odd ball, somebody not really worth bothering with. This was the first time either of them had ever heard him speak and their normally vacant faces expressed that surprise.

The penalty expert, perhaps feeling his title was being irretrievably usurped, was the one who replied.

First of all, what a load of old bollocks.

He became more menacing.

And second, who the fuck asked you, Einstein?

B cowered visibly under the venomously delivered onslaught and lowered his shoulders into his chest, hedgehog-like, to try to make himself less vulnerable to further attack. And then he shuffled off towards the corner where the racing pages of the newspapers were kept on elegant, pale wood poles.

He knew he was right about the penalty kick. Our gift to the world, his father used to say, and we haven't given it much else.

But that knowledge wasn't going to protect him here. He dropped his shoulders even further than before and shrank into himself once again. Trying to hide, always trying to hide. What a talent that would be. Automatic camouflage, the hidden man. He envied with every part of him those who could just disappear at will, fade away from view, escape from the world.

Way back, he remembered reading about George Best doing that kind of disappearing act when he just hid out in a flat belonging to some actress in London. They all knew where he was – his manager, the journalists – but he just locked the door and refused to come out. In on the Friday and nobody saw him until the Monday or the Tuesday. It was in all the papers and even on the television news. Everyone had an opinion about it, usually bad. Around the kitchen table his parents tut-tutted in unison.

> All that talent and he's just throwing it all away. If I had a tenth of what he has I wouldn't waste it like that.

His mother agreed with his father.

> It's his parents I feel sorry for. Sitting having to watch all that. Just an embarrassment really.

B looked at them and had never felt as distant and removed from them in all of his life. He understood completely why Best had done it and why he continued to try to escape from the world. You don't like what you see, what's been offered to you, and you get as far away from it as possible. Simple stuff.

After everything that he had seen and after everything that they had done to him, it was attractive beyond belief for B to disappear. All he needed now was a young good-looking actress with a spare room and curtains on the windows. He smiled to himself and enjoyed the fact that even if they guessed for a million years his mother and father couldn't find out what he was really thinking.

There was no-one to do anything for him now. He knew that. Everyone and everything he loved or had was gone. All that he had seen, all that they had done. That was all that was left now.

Could it have been different if he had just spoken up? They all wanted Witness B to come forward and do the right thing. Whatever that might have been. He was Witness B. That much he knew. Now that all of this was crumbling and falling away, Witness B, being Witness B, was all of him that really remained. It was who he was and who he would be.

Maybe it wasn't too late to do something. That might help. He didn't know. But it was never going to happen. That much he was now sure of. They were all dead anyway. The man on the street. His parents.

Probably even the men who did it. The cruellest trick of all was that he was now the one who had to carry it around, this weight, this burden. All on his own.

There would be no help from anyone else. Just him, just him. Witness B. Deep down he knew this was how it was going to finish. Deep down he knew there was no alternative.

One more bet and then home. The smell of victory that would keep him going back, on Monday, next Saturday and on and on. The Paddy Power Handicap Chase was just as difficult to figure out as it looked. Twenty runners. None of them superstars and some right donkeys down near the bottom of the pile.

As he scanned down the form and the weights, the bottom horse caught his eye. Granit Jack was running for the first time this season, trained by Paul Nicholls and ridden by Ruby Walsh. He must have had some sweat to get down to 10 stone, so there had to be something in that at least. It was good enough for B anyway.

He scribbled out his bet. A £2 win at 7/2. He took the price because with Ruby it was more likely to come in than go out and he wanted to get the best value. After shuffling across to the Bet window, head down to the floor, B wordlessly handed his slip over to the disinterested woman behind the counter. She managed to keep checking the texts on the phone in her left hand while putting the bet through the machine with her right. She didn't even lift her head as she handed the duplicate back to him.

As the race unfolded, B watched the screen, cold and detached. Life was happening all around him but not in him, not to him. Granit Jack was barely mentioned by the commentator. The race was won by one of Ferdy Murphy's.

B felt nothing as the horses trundled past the finishing post. Without looking down he tore up the losing betting slip, first in two and then into a succession of smaller pieces. When they would not divide any more, he allowed the fragments to drop to the floor. They fell like icing sugar being sieved on top of a cooling cake.

END